LOVE
THE LORD
YOUR GOD

A 30-DAY DEVOTIONAL ON
CHRIST'S GREATEST COMMANDMENTS

LOVE
THE LORD
YOUR GOD

**A 30-DAY DEVOTIONAL ON
CHRIST'S GREATEST COMMANDMENTS**

TABLE OF CONTENTS

INTRODUCTION

In Mark 12, a scribe approaches Jesus to ask a seemingly unanswerable question: of all God's commandments, which is the greatest? Christ's reply is short and to the point, citing Deuteronomy 6:4–5 in responding "Hear, O Israel: The Lord our God, the Lord is one. And you shall love the Lord your God with all your heart and with all your soul and with all your mind and with all your strength."

But he didn't stop there.

He continued—unprompted—by adding "The second is this: 'You shall love your neighbor as yourself.'"

But what does it mean to love God and our neighbor as the Lord describes? After all, if these commands truly do form the foundation for "all the Law and the Prophets," then we need to get them right.

Starting with what the Bible means when it calls us to love, in this study we will take those concepts and apply them to an understanding of how we are to love God and neighbor in order to learn how we can do both more reliably and in accordance with his will.

Our goal, however, is to go deeper than simple understanding.

Each day's devotional will invite you to spend time in prayer and reflection, seeking to discern not only what it means to love as the Lord requires but also why doing so consistently can be so difficult.

There tends to be something in our fallen humanity that pushes back on the idea of surrendering ourselves completely to another being, even if it's God. Yet, such surrender is key to the love that God is looking for.

He knows it won't be easy, though, which is part of why he chose to love us first.

You see, God was well within his rights to require our loyalty and devotion for the simple fact that he is God. But while he is worthy of such things, they would not yield the kind of relationship he wants with us. So rather than start with demands that we love him, he chose to begin by loving us.

And, knowing that we are inclined to forget that basic fact, he grounds these commands in reminders of all the ways that he has proven that love throughout our history.

In Deuteronomy, it's by calling his people to remember how he saved them from Egypt and the promise of leading them to the place of abundance and blessing that he had sworn to give their ancestors. However, the greatest demonstration of God's love for us came in Jesus, who died for us while we were still his enemies.

If there has ever been a being worthy of our complete devotion and boundless love, it's God. And he asks us to take the love we have for him and extend it to our neighbor as well.

Let's start today.

WHAT DOES IT MEAN TO LOVE?

In our culture, few concepts have been misunderstood and misappropriated as much as the idea of what it means to love. So when Jesus calls us to love God with our heart, soul, mind, and strength, and our neighbor as ourself, it can be difficult to understand what all that entails.

Luckily, in Christ we find a perfect example of what biblical love looks like. In this section, we will take a look at the way Jesus loved people to better understand how we are called to love in return.

And that starts by understanding that love is a choice rather than an emotion.

One of the most difficult aspects of loving God and loving others is that there will be times where we simply don't feel like loving anyone. In those circumstances, if love was a natural response to how we felt about another person—or even God—in a given moment, then it would be outside of our control and Christ would be setting us up to fail in commanding that we love God and love our neighbor without exception.

Fortunately, that's not the case.

Because love is a choice, there will never be a time that we cannot love in the way that the Lord requires of us. However, simply gritting our teeth and saying that we care about someone is not what God has in mind either.

What we see in Jesus is an example of boundless love that is genuine and sacrificial, but without losing sight of the fact that—especially when it comes to loving other people—pursuing their greatest good may not always feel loving to them.

We'll expand on each of those thoughts in the devotions that follow, but it's important to go into this discussion with the understanding that loving well is complicated and beyond our capacity to accomplish without the Lord's help.

So, to finish for today, spend some time in prayer.

1. Ask God to prepare you for the discussion to come.

2. Ask him to help you identify any ways in which your concepts of love may differ from what Scripture describes.

3. Finally, make the decision now to submit to what he shows you, knowing that the Lord will never call us to love him or love others in ways he has not first loved us.

4. Take those thoughts and form them into a prayer, then write the prayer down in the space below.

WHAT IS LOVE?

Love is a word that gets thrown around a lot in our culture. As a result, it tends to be a concept we think we understand, if only because we hear about it so much. Unfortunately, that can make it hard for us to square what the Bible teaches with how we're inclined to think about it.

So, before we dive further into what it means to love, take a few moments to reflect on how love is typically portrayed in our culture.

1. Write down a few of the key qualities that often define how our culture understands the concept of love today.

With those answers in mind, lets take a closer look at how the Bible defines love in order to compare the two understandings.

HOW GOD DEFINES LOVE

While the Bible defines love in a variety of ways across the breadth of God's word, a common thread is that biblical love prioritizes the pursuit of another person's well-being over your own.

Now, that does not mean we ignore our own needs or diminish ourselves in order to lift others up. No good parent wants that for their children, and the same is true of our heavenly Father. But knowing where to draw that line can be difficult, and Scripture doesn't advocate for an easy, one-size-fits-all approach to how we should love others.

Rather, God's plan is for the practical ways in which we love to be part of an ongoing conversation with him.

In short, the Holy Spirit gets to be the one who decides what it means for us to love others and to love him, and our primary job is to follow his guidance.

2. What is your first reaction when you read that God dictates what it means to love?

3. What are some practical ways in which the biblical approach to loving others differs from the approach of the culture as you described it above?

LOVE IS NOT A FEELING

Though we are ultimately called to follow God's lead on what it means to love in a given situation, his word gives us some general guidelines.

Perhaps the most significant difference between the culture's understanding of love and the understanding we find in the Bible is that, in Scripture, love is a choice rather than an emotion.

God never commands us how to feel. He does not designate certain emotions as inherently sinful or others as necessarily pure. Rather, his primary concern is with how we respond to those emotions.

Love is much the same.

God can command us to love him (Deuteronomy 6:5), to love our enemies (Matthew 5:44), and to love others as ourselves (Mark 12:31) because it is always within our power to do so. Were love synonymous with affection or desire, then it would be beyond our ability to control and, as such, there would be times where we were incapable of following Christ's commands.

God does not set us up to fail like that. He knows that we will sin, but we will never encounter a situation in which we have no option except to sin.

Understanding this distinction is important because it removes one of the primary barriers to loving people well: the belief that we have to like them first.

That may sound harsh, but if we wait to love our enemies until we can convince ourselves that we like our enemies, then chances are that we're never going to start loving them or liking them. And the same logic extends to all of our relationships.

After a big fight, most spouses do not feel very loving toward one another. And every parent can remember a time when their child was jumping on their last nerve like it was a trampoline. You may not *like* the other person in those moments, but it doesn't mean that you stopped loving them.

Why? Because love is a choice you make that goes beyond fickle feelings like warmth and agreeableness. In those moments, the best way to honor the other person as God intends is to remember your decision to prioritize their best interests and act accordingly.

IF OUR LOVE FOR GOD IS *LIMITED* BY HOW MUCH
WE LIKE HIM, THEN WE WILL NOT BE ABLE TO
CONSISTENTLY DEDICATE OUR *HEART, SOUL, MIND, AND
STRENGTH* TO HIS SERVICE. WE WILL NOT BE ABLE TO
LOVE HIM AS THE BIBLE DESCRIBES AND AS HE DESERVES.

4. Take a moment to reflect on a time when you failed to love someone when you did not particularly like them. What factors led to that decision?

5. Next, think back on a time when you chose to love someone well when you did not like them. What factors led to that decision? How did those factors differ from the previous question?

WHEN YOU DON'T LIKE GOD

While it's important to remember that love is a choice in our relationships with other people, it is just as important (if not more) to remember that love is a choice in our relationship with God.

There will be times in life when it feels like God has let us down. Whether it's an issue we face personally, something that afflicts a loved one, or even just looking at the depravity and evil in the world around us, there will be days when we have difficulty reconciling God's omnipotent, omniscient, all-loving nature with the difficulties inherent to this life.

And in those moments, we may not like God very much.

In fact, we may want nothing more than to vent and scream about all the ways in which we simply cannot understand why he hasn't stepped in to change something that is within his power to change.

If our love for God is limited by how much we like him, then we will not be able to consistently dedicate our heart, soul, mind, and strength to his service. We will not be able to love him as the Bible describes and as he deserves.

And he knows that.

It's why he gives us examples throughout Scripture of people arguing with him or yelling at him without condemning either action.

Now, there's certainly a line we shouldn't cross—he is still God, after all—and if our frustrations turn into disrespect, he can be quick to remind us of that fact. But ultimately, the God who made us knows that there will be times when our finite minds cannot understand his infinite perspective on our lives and that we will be tempted to respond out of frustration more than faith.

Even then, though, he also knows that our best path forward is to prioritize our pursuit of his well-being—which Jesus defines as obedience to his word and will (John 14:15)—even when we may not feel like doing so.

Think of a time when you did not like God very much. How did you respond in that moment? Looking back, would you change anything about that response?

LOOKING TO CHRIST'S EXAMPLE

Whether it's loving God or loving others, doing so consistently is difficult. Fortunately, the Gospels give us an excellent example of what that looks like in Jesus. As he told his disciples, "A new commandment I give to you, that you love one another: just as I have loved you, you also are to love one another" (John 13:34).

To that end, over the next few days we are going to look at examples from Jesus' life for additional characteristics of what the Bible means when it calls us to love. Then, we'll examine what it means to apply those principles to loving God with our heart, soul, mind, and strength and our neighbors as ourselves.

6. As we finish for today, spend a few minutes praying and reflecting on ways that you can choose to love God and those he has brought into your life. Ask the Lord to point out anyone whom you need to love better. Then write down the thoughts the Holy Spirit brings to mind.

7. When you're done, turn those thoughts into a prayer, asking for God's help in loving well the people he brought to mind and any others that you may encounter.

LOVE IS GENUINE

In the last day's discussion, we defined love as the decision to prioritize the pursuit of another's well-being over your own. We also talked about how we can do that regardless of circumstances because love is a choice rather than an emotion. We can love our enemies, love people who don't love us, and even love people when we don't particularly like them because the responsibility to love others lies solely with us.

The same is true with our love for God.

However, our heavenly Father knows that such love does not come naturally to us.

Choosing to think of others before we think of ourselves is hard. Fortunately, he showed us how to love when he became one of us. And while words can never fully express the fullness of Christ's love, certain aspects of how Jesus loved are directly applicable to how we should love God, love others, and receive that love in return.

We're going to look at the first of those characteristics today.

LOVE IS GENUINE

One of the most foundational aspects of Christ's love as revealed in Scripture is that his love for others was genuine. Those he encountered were often drawn to Jesus because there was not a hint of falsehood or deception in the way that he loved people.

Some did not recognize it initially, and many responded to that love by questioning it as a way to avoid dealing with their own issues. Yet, for those who were open to receiving it, they experienced a kind of care and affection that left them feeling truly valued.

1. Can you think of a time when you have encountered that kind of love? If so, what are some of the most enduring impressions you remember? If you can't think of an instance where you experienced that kind of love, will you spend the next few moments instead asking God to help you receive it from him?

LOVE IS TIME

Few things leave as lasting an impression on people as feeling as though they are genuinely cared for. So how did Jesus exhibit such love and how can we learn to do the same?

He started with his time.

One of the earliest examples of Christ's genuine love for others is found toward the end of Luke 4. Jesus had just come to Capernaum in Galilee after being chased out of his hometown of Nazareth for confronting the people with their unbelief. He then spent the morning of the Sabbath teaching in the synagogue and driving a demon out of a man who came to listen. Afterward, he and his disciples went back to Peter's house in the city, where Jesus healed Peter's mother-in-law (Luke 4:31–39).

As Luke describes, "Now when the sun was setting, all those who had any who were sick with various diseases brought them to him, and he laid his hands on every one of them and healed them" (Luke 4:40).

2. When you think of Jesus in this moment, what impressions come to mind?

JESUS NEVER SEEMS TO LOVE OTHERS OUT OF A
SENSE OF *OBLIGATION*. RATHER, HIS COMPULSION
TO CARE FOR THOSE HE MET WAS AN EXTENSION OF
HIS *RELATIONSHIP* WITH THE FATHER. IT WAS IN HIS
NATURE TO LOVE, AND THE MORE WE GROW IN OUR
LOVE FOR HIM, THE MORE IT SHOULD BECOME PART
OF *OUR NATURE* AS WELL (1 JOHN 4:16).

LOVE IS SACRIFICIAL

It can be easy to allow Christ's divinity to overshadow his humanity when we think about his time walking amongst us. After all, driving out demons and performing miracles is hardly something you see every day. However, it's important to remember that while Jesus was also fully divine, the work he did teaching, healing, and ministering to others still took its toll on him.

That's why the next day, he got up and "went into a desolate place" (v. 42). By the time he finally got some space from the crowds, he was so tired that he slept through much of the storm that threatened to sink the ship on which he and his disciples sailed (Matthew 8:23–26).

Understanding the price of Christ's humanity is important because it sheds light on how much it truly cost him to love as he did. We'll look at the sacrificial elements of that love in greater detail tomorrow, but for now we can know that the love Jesus showed to people throughout his ministry was genuine because we know that it was not easy.

That's not to say love always has to be sacrificial to be real love, but there are few ways to more clearly show someone that you are prioritizing their well-being over your own than to make your life more difficult for their benefit.

At the same time, Jesus never seems to love others out of a sense of obligation. Rather, his compulsion to care for those he met was an extension of his relationship with the Father. It was in his nature to love, and the more we grow in our love for him, the more it should become part of our nature as well (1 John 4:16).

3. Think back on the last time it cost you something to love another person. What led you to pay that cost?

4. Did you expect gratitude and a similar act of love in return or was your focus primarily on blessing the other person?

LOVE IS COMPASSIONATE

We see another example of Christ's genuine love when Matthew describes how, when Jesus saw the crowds "throughout all the cities and villages" in which he taught, "he had compassion for them, because they were harassed and helpless, like sheep without a shepherd" (Matthew 9:35–36).

The word in verse 36 often translated as compassion—*esplanchnisthe*—is the deepest form of compassion that could be expressed in the Greek. It more literally refers to the bowels, and the idea is that Christ was moved with a sense of empathy that arose from the very depths of his being.

The word is used several times in the Gospels but, outside of a few parables, never describes anyone other than Christ. At times, it's used to describe the sense of pity or grief he feels for those who are hurting (Matthew 14:14, 20:34). Elsewhere, the gospel writers use it to refer to the empathy he feels for those who are alone (Mark 1:41). And here in Matthew 9, it refers more to the compassion Christ feels for those who are searching but who lack the necessary direction and guidance to find the right path.

In each case, what we see in Jesus is a kind of love motivated by the desire to help those who need it without any hint of selfishness or deception. We can know that love was genuine because Scripture makes clear that it was wholly focused on the needs of the other person and how Jesus could help them.

Such love is no more common today than it was in the first century. What drew the crowds to Jesus then can still draw people to Jesus today when they experience his love through us.

5. When was the last time you experienced this type of compassion?

6. When you think about the way that God loves you, where does such empathy rank on the list of qualities? Why do you think that's the case?

CHRIST'S STANDARD FOR LOVE

This side of heaven, it's unlikely that you and I will ever fully and consistently model the kind of genuine love we see in Christ. However, that is the standard to which we are called, and Jesus was clear that we sin when we stop trying just because we understand that we will fall short (Matthew 5:48).

7. So as we finish for today, take some time to ask God to show you any relationships in your life where you are falling short of the genuine love we see in Jesus. Ask him to point out ways you can love others without thinking of how that love might benefit you. Write down what he brings to mind.

8. Now ask those same questions about your love for him. In what ways is your love for God selfish rather than selfless? How can you show him the same kind of genuine love he has shown you? Write down what he brings to mind.

9. When you're done, turn those thoughts into a prayer, asking for God's help in showing the kind of genuine love toward other people and toward him that we see modeled in the life of Christ. Write down your prayer so that you can return to it as needed across the following days.

LOVE IS SACRIFICIAL

Yesterday we discussed what it means for love to be genuine and how Christ exemplified that type of love through the honest, compassionate way he approached those whom the Father brought along his path. Jesus's desire to care for others contained no hint of obligation or selfishness in its motivation, and the truth of that statement was clear to all who willingly received the love he freely offered. We who are called to extend Christ's love to those we meet today need to follow his example.

However, to love genuinely will, at times, require that we also love sacrificially. Fortunately, we can once again find timeless guidance for what that looks like in the life of Jesus.

LOVE IS SACRIFICIAL

When we reflect on the sacrificial element of Christ's love for us, the cross is often the first example that comes to mind. And for good reason. As Jesus said, "Greater love has no one than this, that someone lay down his life for his friends" (John 15:13). Moreover, Paul adds that we were not even his friends when he made the decision to die on our behalf so that we might have the chance to be restored into a right relationship with God (Romans 5:10).

At the same time, most of us are never going to be called to die so that someone else might live. We cannot know that such a sacrifice will not be required of us, but the odds are against it. So how can we model the sacrificial love of Christ if the greatest example of that love is not something we can really emulate?

The key is found in the larger context of John 15.

Throughout the first seventeen verses of John 15, Jesus speaks of the need to abide consistently in his word and to follow his commandments. He describes a life defined by service and loyalty to the Lord. That call culminates in verses 12–14 when he states, "This is my commandment, that you love one another as I have loved you. Greater love has no one than this, that someone lay down his life for his friends. You are my friends if you do what I command you."

Verse 13 often gets the most notoriety, but the surrounding statements make two clear points:

1. Laying down your life can mean a willingness to die in place of someone else, as Jesus did for us on the cross.

2. More commonly, laying down one's life can also refer to the daily sacrifice of making your desires and wants secondary to the needs of those God brings into your life.

And while it's essential that we allow the Holy Spirit to be the one who guides us in knowing how to meet those needs—after all, another person's need *does not* automatically constitute your calling—Christ's call is for us to give him a blank check in terms of what we are willing to sacrifice when the Lord asks it of us.

1. Take a moment to pray and ask God to help you make a list of the people you genuinely believe you would be willing to die for. Write down their names.

2. Now take some time to ask the Holy Spirit to help you understand the degree to which your daily interactions and devotion to those people exemplify that kind of love. Put another way, to what extent do you make the daily sacrifice of serving the people God brought to mind and meeting their needs ahead of your own?

3. Has your willingness to make the ultimate sacrifice mitigated your commitment to making a daily sacrifice on their behalf?

LOVE IS SELFLESS

The cross, however, is not the only example Jesus gives us of what it means to love sacrificially.

Few stories from his life exemplify this kind of love better than when Jesus, aware that the cross was in his imminent future, chose to stoop down and wash the feet of his disciples.

4. Read John 13:1–17.

5. Now, close your eyes and picture yourself in the place of one of the disciples. See Jesus going down the line, getting closer to you with every passing minute. Now it's your turn. Feel the water pour over your feet. Feel the towel as the God of the universe works to remove the last vestiges of dirt and grime from between your toes. Now look into his eyes as he raises his gaze to meet yours before moving on to the next person.

6. As you reflect on this passage and what it would have been like to be among those whose feet were washed that day, what stands out most about Christ's love for you?

7. What would it look like to love someone else with that same level of selfless devotion?

While there are many aspects of this story that teach us what it means to love sacrificially, one of the most important stems from the fact that Jesus did not have to wash his disciples' feet. In fact, such an action was so far beneath him that his followers were genuinely shocked and, as we see with Peter, initially appalled that he would presume to do so.

But that was the point.

An act is far less sacrificial when it is compelled or done for selfish reasons than when it is done by choice with the primary goal of blessing the other person. Recognizing that distinction when evaluating our motivations is key to loving well. And, as we see from passages like Luke's description of the early church at the end of Acts 2, his disciples came to understand and apply that lesson (vv. 42–47).

One of the primary reasons that having the correct motivations is so important when loving sacrificially is that it can be easy to make such acts of caring about yourself.

It's been said that the best way to know if you have a servant's heart is to watch how you react when someone treats you like a servant. There is a good bit of truth to that sentiment. Ultimately, if we are loving others with the expectation that such love will be returned to us, then we are in danger of loving selfishly rather than sacrificially.

Now, that doesn't mean love ceases to be sacrificial if it's reciprocated. Such reciprocity is how love should work.

If we all loved each other sacrificially, as Jesus commands, then we would all experience a level of love that far surpasses anything else we could hope to receive. But it's not always going to work out that way. And, if we're going to follow Christ's example, the other person's response cannot factor into how far we are willing to follow the Holy Spirit's guidance in loving others.

If such love ever seems too difficult or unreasonable, just remember that Jesus washed Judas's feet that day as well, knowing that at least some of the mud he was cleaning off likely came from the road Judas took to arrange Christ's betrayal (Matthew 26:14–16).

SACRIFICIAL LOVE IS FOUNDATIONAL

Ultimately, a willingness to love sacrificially is foundational to our ability to love God with our heart, soul, mind, and strength and to love our neighbor as ourselves.

But as we said at the beginning, such love is hard. It requires making a daily commitment to surrender every facet of our lives to the Holy Spirit's guidance. It means loving others even if they can't or won't love us in return. And it entails seeing that love as an extension of our service to the Lord in gratitude for the love he has first shown us.

8. If you made an honest assessment of how you love God on a day-to-day basis, to what extent would you describe that love as sacrificial? When you fall short of that standard, what are the primary reasons why?

9. Now ask those same questions about your love for others. Where do the answers differ? Where are they the same?

As we conclude for today, take a few minutes to ask the Lord to help you understand how to love more sacrificially, both in your relationship with him and in your interactions with other people. Be specific in response to what he showed you in the previous reflections.

10. When you're done, turn those thoughts into a prayer and write it down in the space below.

DAY 5

LOVE IS ACCOUNTABLE

Yesterday we discussed what it means to love sacrificially and studied the example of Christ to better understand what that looks like. One of the key components of such sacrifice is that we take on that cost without thought to whether such love will be reciprocated. Blessing the other person becomes a higher priority than receiving a blessing in return. That principle is key to understanding the last of the characteristics we will discuss in this section regarding what it means to love.

LOVE IS ACCOUNTABLE

One of the most damaging misappropriations of Christ's love in our culture today is the idea that Jesus just wanted us to care for and appreciate other people without regard for their sin. To be sure, Jesus did not make adherence to biblical morality a necessary precursor to the mercy and kindness he often showed to people throughout his ministry. However, he also made it clear that they could never receive the fullness of his love if they chose to remain more committed to their sin than to repentance.

Such accountability is not always seen as compatible with love. However, that reality speaks primarily to a modern misunderstanding of what it means to love well.

Only telling people what they want to hear rather than risking their ire to confront them with the truth they need to hear is one of the most selfish and unloving actions we can take in our relationships with other people. Now, we must be wary of approaching such accountability in unloving ways, something that Christ's example can help us avoid. But we must never let the fear of another person's response keep us from obeying God's call to help people face the reality of their sin and, in repentance, leave it behind to turn and run toward the grace and salvation our heavenly Father offers.

But before we take a closer look at how Jesus exemplified a loving accountability in his interactions with others, it's necessary to take a few moments to understand how we respond to this kind of accountability, since it is often far easier to give than to receive.

1. Take a few minutes to pray and ask the Holy Spirit to bring to mind times when other people have pointed out sin in your life. What was your initial reaction? What factors influenced the degree to which you were willing to accept their accountability?

2. Now ask yourself the same questions about times when that accountability has come from the Holy Spirit's conviction in your life. What, if anything, is different about your reaction when your shortcomings are pointed out by God rather than other people?

Appreciating and remembering how difficult it can be to receive criticism is a necessary first step to giving such criticism well. Toward the end of today's devotion, we'll look at why that truth is important in loving God, but it's equally important in understanding how to love other people. To that end, let's look at how Jesus held people accountable in a way that demonstrated his deep and abiding love for them.

HOW DO YOU DEFINE OTHERS?

In John 8:2–11, we find Jesus teaching people at the temple in Jerusalem. In the middle of his lesson, the religious leaders interrupted Jesus by bringing before him a woman caught in adultery.[1] They cited Moses's command in Deuteronomy 22:22 that a woman caught in adultery should be stoned, and asked Jesus his opinion on the matter. That the man with whom she committed adultery was left alone, despite that same passage in Deuteronomy calling for him to be killed as well, provides important context for their actions.

However, if any doubt remained as to why the religious leaders brought the woman before Jesus, verse 6 explains their motivations clearly: "This they said to test him, that they might have some charge to bring against him."

For their question to Jesus to be a trap, however, they had to go into it expecting Jesus to show the woman a level of mercy that exceeded their understanding of the law.

You see, mercy was such a fundamental part of Christ's character and ministry that the religious leaders knew he would not condemn this woman according to their rules. However, what they saw as a negative was always God's true purpose for the law: to remind us of both the standards to which we are called to live and also our inability to meet them apart from his help. The way Christ showed mercy to the woman who needed it while also calling her to "go, and from now on sin no more" (John 8:11) encapsulated that balance and defined much of his ministry.

When we think about loving others by helping them to repent of their sin and embrace a life of holiness, how closely do we align with Christ? Do people automatically get defensive around us because they expect a lecture and condemnation? Or are they willing to listen because they know the call to "sin no more" is accompanied by a loving acceptance of who they are as a person made in the image of God?

To put it another way, what defines people in our eyes? Is it their sin, or is it their status as someone for whom Jesus died? In either case, their sin needs to be addressed, but we are far more likely to do so in a way that honors God and draws people closer to him when that accountability comes in love rather than judgment.

But it does still need to come.

---

1   The earliest manuscripts do not include this passage in John 8, which is why many modern translations put it in brackets with a note to that effect. It was most likely a story passed down through oral tradition that was added here at a later date. We have included it here because it is still a powerful example of Christ's love that has been studied and applied for the vast majority of Christian history. Moreover, the final words of John's Gospel make clear that "there are also many other things that Jesus did. Were every one of them to be written, I suppose that the world itself could not contain the books that would be written" (John 21:25). As such, there is good reason to believe that the story is genuine, even if its place in John's Gospel is not.

3. When you think about holding others accountable for their sin, what emotions accompany that action? Do you get excited about the prospect of pointing out sin in the lives of others? Does that notion make you uncomfortable and wary? Or do you fall somewhere in between?

4. Take a few moments and ask the Spirit to help you understand your heart and mind on this matter. Why did you answer the previous question as you did? Is there an experience from the past that comes to mind that helps explain that answer? Do you feel like it's just how you're wired?

Understanding what motivates your approach to confronting people with their sin and calling them to a life of repentance is crucial to loving them well. However, those same factors are also crucial to how we love God.

DO YOU RECEIVE ACCOUNTABILITY FROM GOD?

Considering that God is without sin, it will never fall to us to convict him of it or call him to repentance. So, you might be wondering why we chose to include this element of what it means to love in an examination of how to love God with all our heart, soul, mind, and strength.

The answer is that one of the most frequent impediments we will face in our desire to love God well is an inability to receive accountability from him.

Because the Lord is perfect and desires for us to be as well, any unrepentant sin in our lives will necessarily limit the degree to which we can be in a right relationship with him.

Think about it this way: If you are a parent and one of your kids does something wrong, yet they act as though their sin should have no bearing on your relationship going forward, would you be OK with that?

What if it were someone else who sinned against someone you love—as is the case with our heavenly Father whenever our actions hurt another person? If they then tried to ask something of you or acted as though it was no big deal, would you ignore what they'd done?

In the same way, we should not expect God to ignore our sin. If it feels as though the Lord is distant despite your genuine attempts to love him, perhaps it's because he wants to discuss some sin in your life first.

Such accountability is an inseparable part of God's love for us, so receiving it well needs to be foundational to our love for him. And when we do that, we will be better equipped to go forward and call others to a similar repentance because we will understand more deeply how important it is to receive God's love in turn.

5. Take some time to pray and ask God to reveal any sin in your life that currently stands as an impediment to receiving his love and loving him well in return. Fight the urge to get defensive or explain away whatever issues he brings to mind. Instead, embrace the accountability, repent, and ask him to help you understand both how those sins became an issue and what you can do to avoid them going forward.

WHEN YOU IGNORE SIN

Even though God has called us to perfection, he knows we will not achieve it this side of heaven. As a result, what you just prayed needs to be a regular part of your time with him. All of us have sins to which we are particularly vulnerable. Chances are that yours will continue to be a problem even though you have asked for his help with understanding and avoiding them.

And remember, God doesn't love you any less because of your sin. You are still his beloved child for whom he died, and that will always remain the primary lens through which he sees you. However, you can neither receive nor reciprocate that love to its fullest extent if you ignore sin of any kind in your life.

6. So, as we finish for today, take some time to reflect on that truth and write down any thoughts that come to mind.

7. Now turn those thoughts into a prayer, asking God to help you receive and give his love by addressing sin when you see it, either in your life or in the lives of others. And particularly with the latter, ask the Holy Spirit to guide you in knowing how to confront that sin with grace and love rather than judgment.

LOVE IN FULL

Over the past five days, we've examined how the Bible defines love, particularly in contrast to the way it's often understood in the larger culture. We've focused on how the biblical definition entails prioritizing the well-being and interests of another over your own desires, while also noting that such efforts must always remain under the guidance of the Holy Spirit. Apart from that guidance, we open ourselves up to a spectrum of mistakes, from being taken advantage of by those we endeavor to treat well to only loving others when it seems personally beneficial.

Most of us exist somewhere between those two poles, but loving God and others well requires that we approach every situation as a unique opportunity to serve the Lord through the way we love. To that end, we looked at principles from the life of Christ to help us identify some of the core characteristics of how Jesus loved and, from his example, learn how we might apply those lessons in our lives today.

With that goal in mind, let's spend the rest of today looking back on what God has taught us about how to love before shifting the conversation to a more focused examination of what it looks like to love God with our heart, soul, mind, and strength and our neighbor as ourselves. The purpose of such reflection is less to remind you of what we've only recently discussed than to revisit those ideas in light of the ones that followed.

While each of the following characteristics is important in its own right, they build on one another to present a more cohesive look at what it means to love. If we do not have a solid understanding of the picture they present as a whole, then it will matter relatively little whether we master the individual parts.

LOVE IS GENUINE

The first characteristic we discussed is how Christ's love is genuine. Jesus loved without the slightest hint of falsehood or deception, and that was true of every interaction he had with people throughout the Gospels. He gave freely of his time and efforts as the Spirit led, and as a result, those who experienced his love often left those interactions with a renewed sense of their worth in the eyes of God.

1. Take a few minutes to look back over the questions we discussed in the devotional on what it means for our love to be genuine (day 3). Would you answer those questions any differently today than when you first considered them?

2. In your own words, write down what it means to love genuinely based on the example of Jesus. How closely does your love for others adhere to that definition?

LOVE IS SACRIFICIAL

The second characteristic we discussed is that Christ's love is sacrificial.

While the cross is the ultimate example of that sacrifice, Jesus's interactions with others demonstrated that such love was not limited to that single act. Each day he exhibited the same kind of selfless concern for others that led him to die in our place, and he calls us to do the same. From washing his disciples' feet—including the feet of Judas—to the way he healed and taught even while exhausted, Christ gave us a clear example of what it looks like to love sacrificially.

3. Take a few minutes to look back over the questions we discussed in the devotional on what it means for our love to be sacrificial (day 4). Would you answer those questions any differently today than when you first considered them? Has your understanding of what it means to love genuinely changed the way you understand what it means to love sacrificially?

4. In your own words, write down what it means to love sacrificially based on the example of Jesus. How closely does your love for others adhere to that definition?

LOVE IS ACCOUNTABLE

The final characteristic of Christ's love we discussed is the way he confronted people with their sin and called them to repentance. However, his life was so defined by grace and mercy that, even when calling people to go and sin no more, they understood that he did so to set them free rather than to condemn them. Such a balance is not possible unless our love for others is both genuine and sacrificial.

Because such accountability will often breed a sense of defensiveness on the part of those who are confronted with their mistakes, they have to trust that we really do have their ultimate well-being in mind. However, even when our motivations are genuine, it does not guarantee that others will accept that accountability well. The willingness to risk their wrath and ire to help them draw closer to God by choosing his mercy over their sin is an inherently sacrificial act. If we are not willing to suffer the consequences of rejected accountability, then we will never offer it well.

5. With those factors in mind, take a few minutes to look back over the questions we discussed in the devotional on what it means for our love to be accountable (day 5). Would you answer those questions any differently today than when you first considered them? Has your understanding of what it means to love both genuinely and sacrificially changed the way you understand what it means to love by calling others to repentance?

6. In your own words, write down what it means for love to be accountable based on the example of Jesus. How closely does your love for others adhere to that definition?

HOW THE TRINITY REVEALS HOW TO LOVE

To this point, much of our conversation has centered on what it means to love other people, which may come as a surprise considering that the primary emphasis of this resource is how to love God. Here too, the example of Jesus can help.

Christ's love for other people was, in many ways, an extension of his love for the Father.

The paradox of the Trinity is the question of how God can be three distinct persons who equally share the divine nature of what it means to be God. Over the course of Christian history, there have been those who sought to understand this paradox by arguing for some form of the heresy known as adoptionism or modalism. In this understanding, the three persons of the Trinity are essentially just God wearing different masks.

While this argument has been understood from the start to be a heresy, it still pops up from time to time under different names. It's relevant to our discussion today because, if it were true, then the love Jesus shows for the Father would really just be a self-interested and deceptive love for himself.

That is not what we see in the Bible.

When Jesus speaks of the respect, loyalty, and love he has for the Father, his commitment is genuine. Moreover, though he was fully God, he chose to prioritize the will of the Father and frequently spoke about how he had not come "to do my own will but the will of him who sent me" (John 6:38). And while Christ's sinless existence meant there was never a time when he had to be held accountable by the Father, his love was such that it seems clear he would have prioritized being in a right relationship with him over a prideful resentment of criticism.

In short, the genuine, sacrificial, and accountable love we see Jesus display toward other people is mirrored in his love for the Father. The same should be true of us as well.

If we want to love God with our heart, soul, mind, and strength, then we must also be willing to love our neighbor as ourselves. For the latter to be consistent and true to what we find in Scripture, though, it must flow out of our love for God.

So, as we conclude this first section, take some time to reflect on the Bible's definition of love.

7. In what ways does the biblical definition of love vary from what you've seen in the culture or experienced from other people?

8. In what ways has your understanding of what it means to love evolved from when our conversation began?

9. And of the three characteristics discussed in this section, which do you struggle the most with?

Write down your answers to these questions and, when you're done, turn those thoughts into a prayer asking God to help you remember what it means to love well.

HOW TO LOVE GOD WITH ALL YOUR HEART

In our culture today, the heart is most often associated with our emotions. However, that was not the case in biblical times. In Jewish thought, emotions were more commonly associated with the soul, while the heart was seen as the part of a person's being that made decisions.

As a result, loving God with all our heart means making the choice to love him, regardless of our circumstances or what that love might require of us. Unfortunately, that's often easier said than done.

That's why, in this section, we're going to look for guidance on what it means to love God with all our heart from a series of biblical figures.

Through Moses, we learn about what it means to love God by obeying God, while Pharaoh stands as a somber warning of how quickly our disobedience can harden our hearts to the Lord.

From there, we'll look to David for guidance on how to love God with our affections rather than our emotions, noting how our affections serve as a more consistent foundation for our relationship with him, since they are not as reliant upon the whims of feeling.

That consistency is especially important given that there will be plenty of times when circumstances make it hard to feel overly fond of others, even God. However, if you are committed to loving someone, then your circumstances won't diminish that love—something that Job demonstrates throughout the book that bears his name.

Last, we'll spend some time wrestling with what Paul means when he writes of learning to be content in all circumstances and consider how that sense of contentment rests upon the aspects of loving God with our heart that we'll study in the coming days.

Our discussion will conclude with looking at how loving God with our heart serves as the foundation for loving our neighbor in the same way. Just as we are to love God with a consistency and affection that goes beyond our feelings and circumstances, Christ calls us to love others in the same way. However, we will fail in the latter unless that love flows out from the love we have for God.

We'll explore that basic truth in each of the following sections as well, noting how loving God with your soul, mind, and strength are equally important for the task of loving your neighbor as yourself.

But, before we do, let's take a moment to pray.

1. Ask God to help you understand any way in which your heart is not aligned with his.

2. Ask him to identify any ways in which your circumstances might be affecting your love for the Lord.

3. Finish by turning those thoughts into a prayer, and write it down so you can return to what the Lord has shown you across the coming days.

LOVING GOD WITH YOUR HEART

Because, as we've discussed previously, love is primarily a choice rather than an emotion, it is always within our power to love as Scripture commands. That element of choice is crucial to understanding what it means to love God in every respect, but it's particularly important when it comes to loving God with our heart.

In Jewish thought, the heart was not simply the seat of emotions. Rather, it was the center of a person's being, the place from which they made decisions. In many ways, the Hebrew understanding of the heart was similar to the Greek understanding of the mind, which we will examine in greater detail when we look at what it means to love God with our mind. For now, our focus will remain on what it means to love the Lord with our heart.

"IF YOU LOVE ME . . ."

When God commanded Israel to love him with their hearts, one of the key elements was demonstrating their love through obedience.

Jesus reiterated this concept when he told his disciples "If you love me, you will keep my commandments," adding a few verses later that "whoever has my commandments and keeps them, he it is who loves me. And he who loves me will be loved by my Father, and I will love him and manifest myself to him" (John 14:15, 21).

The concepts of love and obedience are intricately linked throughout the biblical narrative, and that connection is just as important for us as it was for ancient Israel and those first generations of Christians.

1. When you think about the connection between love and obedience, what is your first reaction to the concept?

2. Does such obedience seem like a natural way to love? Or does part of you resist the idea?

Every person reacts to the idea of obeying another—even when it's God—in their own way, and the Lord knows that. After all, he's the one who wired each of us to be unique individuals rather than a uniform collective.

One thing that will become clear the more we explore the concept of loving the Lord with our heart, soul, mind, and strength is that some facets of that calling will feel more natural to you than others. And that's all right.

What we must guard against, however, is the temptation to think we can compensate for deficiencies in one area by leaning into our strengths in another. As will become clear, each area is essential to a well-rounded and intimate relationship with the Lord, and allowing ourselves to settle for less than the standards to which we are called will always yield damaging results.

And the more often we allow ourselves to settle below that standard, the more damaging those results will become. Few stories illustrate that truth as well as the twin stories of Pharaoh and Moses in Exodus.

ONE THING THAT WILL BECOME CLEAR THE
MORE WE EXPLORE THE CONCEPT OF *LOVING
THE LORD* WITH OUR HEART, SOUL, MIND, AND
STRENGTH IS THAT SOME FACETS OF THAT
CALLING WILL FEEL MORE *NATURAL* TO YOU
THAN OTHERS. AND THAT'S ALL RIGHT.

WHO HARDENED PHARAOH'S HEART?

Few biblical characters are aligned more closely with a single characteristic as Pharaoh is with a hardened heart. But what does it mean to have a hardened heart? After all, Scripture speaks of it in different yet seemingly interchangeable ways.

For example, God warns Moses that Pharaoh will not listen to his entreaties to let the Hebrews go because "I will harden Pharaoh's heart, and though I multiply my signs and wonders in the land of Egypt, Pharaoh will not listen to you" (Exodus 7:3–4).

However, in the next chapter Scripture speaks of how Pharaoh "hardened his heart and would not listen to them" (Exodus 8:15). After the next plague, Scripture once again assigns responsibility to Pharaoh instead of God (v. 32). This back and forth continues throughout the narrative.

So which is it? Did God harden Pharaoh's heart, or did that responsibility ultimately reside with the Egyptian ruler?

In truth, we don't know, and the answer is likely a bit of both. It seems clear, however, that Pharaoh was already inclined to say no to God whenever he asked something of him. As a result, whether the state of Pharaoh's heart was a consequence of God's intervention or simply solidifying the king's existing predilections, the end result was likely to be the same. And therein lies the most valuable lesson his example has to teach us.

Like Pharaoh, the more often we tell God no, the harder it will become to eventually say yes. Every time we choose to obey our will rather than the Lord's, our hearts become a little more hardened against him.

That said, none of us can harden our hearts so much that we are beyond the reach of the Lord. We should never give up on ourselves or those around us, no matter how lost they may seem. However, every step away from God can feel as though it takes two to get back, and this need to allow the Spirit to soften what our sin has hardened is a big reason why.

3. Take a few moments to prayerfully reflect on a time when it felt like you were walking away from God. What choices led you down that path? Did you take it in big leaps or small steps?

MOSES WASN'T A YES MAN UNTIL HE WAS

In contrast to Pharaoh, we have the example of Moses. It's worth noting that Moses was not afraid to disagree with God. There were many times—from his initial call in the desert to the plagues in Egypt and on through the Hebrews' trek in the wilderness— where Moses argued against what the Lord was either planning to do or had told him to do. But what sets him apart is that when God finally made known that his will would not change, Moses consented to do it.

In short, Moses made a habit of saying yes to God, even if that assent was preceded by some arguments and debate.

When we think about what it means to love God with our heart today, that is the pattern we should strive to follow. Our heavenly Father isn't asking for a blind, unthinking obedience, though there will be times when we are asked to follow his will without a complete understanding of what that entails. Rather, he invites us to "reason together" and bring our questions to him (Isaiah 1:18). Many of the Psalms penned by a man after God's own heart tell the story of someone struggling to understand and accept the Lord's will before ultimately deciding to do so.

That decision to say yes, even—and especially—when it is difficult, is a key component of what it means to love God with all our heart. It means making the choice to use the freedom he has given us to surrender our will to his.

And just as saying no hardens our heart against the Lord, saying yes softens it, making it all that much easier to say yes in the future as well.

4. Just as you previously took time to reflect on an example of when you said no to God, now think back to a time when you told him yes, even if it was difficult to do so. What factors led you to make that decision? What impact did that moment of obedience have on your relationship with the Lord?

START WITH OBEDIENCE

Ultimately, loving God with all our heart is about more than just obedience, but obedience is where it needs to start. After all, love tends to come naturally when we can see how it is in our best interest. It's the times when loving another is difficult that such love is most powerfully demonstrated.

Tomorrow, we will examine that distinction through the lens of loving God with our affections rather than our emotions. However, to do that well, we must enter into a relationship already committed to obeying the Lord, even when it's difficult. Our hearts are still often the place from which we make our choices, and deciding that those choices will go in accordance with God's will is a crucial first step.

5. Take some time to pray and ask the Lord to help you understand how readily you are willing to obey him. When you do obey, do you see such obedience more as the reluctant recognition that God is God or as an act of love? God is looking for the latter, which is one of the primary reasons he gave us the power to make that choice rather than forcing obedience upon us.

6. So, as we finish for today, take those thoughts and form them into a prayer. Write it down so you can look back on it later.

AFFECTION VERSUS EMOTION

Yesterday, we looked at loving God through obedience. Since, in the Hebrew perspective, the heart was seen as the place from which a person makes decisions, choosing to follow his will—especially when it differed from your own—was a clear indication of love. However, simply choosing to do what God asks of us is not the entirety of what it means to love him with our heart.

Few who have experienced real love, whether given or received, would argue that it is completely within the realm of reason. True love is often accompanied by strong feelings because that's how God designed it.

However, we get into trouble when we allow those feelings to be our guide on how to love rather than the result of it. A more biblical way to think about the role of such feelings when applied to loving God—and, by extension, other people—is to see them as affections rather than emotions.

Jonathan Edwards describes the distinction between affection and emotion well when he writes "The affections and passions are frequently spoken of as the same; and yet in the more common use of speech, there is in some respect a difference; and affection is a word that in its ordinary signification, seems to be something more extensive than passion, being used for all vigorous lively actings of the will or inclination; but passion for those that are more sudden, and whose effects on the animal spirits are more violent, and the mind more overpowered, and less in its own command."

In short, affections are a response, while emotions—or passions, as Edwards calls them—are a reaction.

1. Take a moment to reflect on the difference between affections and emotions, and the role both have played in your relationships. What are some of the primary differences you've seen in how you relate to other people and to God when each was the driving force?

2. What were some of the pros and cons of each?

Practically speaking, one of the greatest distinctions between affections and emotions is that we have more control over the former because they are less likely to be based on spur-of-the-moment feelings. By contrast, emotions are most often the result of whether we like or dislike something in a given moment. As such, our emotions are by nature less consistent and less reliable than our affections.

This distinction is particularly important when it comes to loving God.

DAVID'S AFFECTIONS FOR GOD IN PSALM 27

Some of the best examples we see in Scripture of loving God with your affections rather than your emotions are found in the Psalms, particularly those from David.

3. Take a few minutes to read Psalm 27. What stands out most about the way David speaks of the Lord across these verses? How would you describe his love for God?

Psalm 27 illustrates four important aspects of what it means to love God with our affections.

DAVID HAD A HISTORY OF GOD'S FAITHFULNESS

First, David shows a clear understanding of God's character born from David's personal experiences with the Lord.

He can speak of the security and trust he has in God because he has experienced the Lord's provision (v. 1). In the same way, he can write of evildoers and adversaries falling because he has encountered God's protection in those areas (vv. 2–3). And he picks up on these themes again in verses 5 and 6.

What makes that possible, though, is that David does not take those past experiences for granted. Rather, the lessons he's learned stayed with him and impacted his understanding of God's character long after the initial events faded. They became an integral part of his affection for the Lord.

In the same way, a key element of loving God with all our heart is thinking back on the times he's proven himself faithful and worthy of that love. When those experiences become a foundational part of who we understand the Lord to be, it becomes easier to maintain our affection toward him.

And, as we'll see in a few moments, those connections are crucial because we will also encounter times when experiences may cause us to doubt the Lord's goodness.

4. Take a few moments to pray and ask the Lord to bring to mind examples from your past where you experienced God's goodness. Such reflection is not intended to minimize the times when that goodness may have appeared lacking, as we will discuss later in this devotional. But all of us have encountered some measure of God's grace and love in this life, no matter how difficult the dark times have been.

5. Before moving on to the next part of this devotional, take a moment to write down those good experiences and thank God for them.

DAVID GENUINELY DELIGHTED IN GOD'S PRESENCE

The second element of Psalm 27 that speaks to loving God with our affections is the way David takes genuine delight in the prospect of being in the Lord's presence.

In verse 4 he writes, "One thing have I asked of the Lord, that will I seek after: that I may dwell in the house of the LORD all the days of my life." One of David's strongest sources of joy is the prospect of dwelling with God. There is a clear sense of genuine longing simply to be with the Lord.

It would be difficult to say that you truly loved someone if you did not enjoy spending time with them. Now, that doesn't necessarily mean all the time, as David describes here, because all of us need a break sometimes (especially when it comes to other people). But that basic principle applies to loving God as well.

IF THE THOUGHT OF SPENDING TIME IN PRAYER, READING YOUR BIBLE, OR ANY OF THE OTHER WAYS WE *COMMUNE* WITH THE LORD FEELS MORE LIKE A CHORE THAN SOMETHING THAT EXCITES YOU, THEN IT COULD BE A SIGN THAT YOUR *AFFECTIONS* FOR GOD ARE LACKING AND THE LOVE YOU HAVE TOWARD HIM IS BORN MORE OUT OF *OBLIGATION* THAN *RELATIONSHIP*.

If the thought of spending time in prayer, reading your Bible, or in any of the other ways we commune with the Lord feels more like a chore than something that excites you, then it could be a sign that your affections for God are lacking and the love you have toward him is born more out of obligation than relationship.

To be sure, there are times when we all feel like that—which is an important reason why loving God with our feelings is a bad idea—but we should strive for the kind of relationship with the Lord where coming into his presence feels like we're going home. Praying should impart a sense of peace and joy, even if the rest of our world feels like it's crashing down around us.

We cannot develop that kind of relationship with God overnight any more than we can with another person, but over time it can—and should—come to define what it means for us to enter the Lord's presence.

6. How close are you to experiencing that kind of relationship with God?

If it feels a long way off, do not be discouraged. Guilt is not a feeling that comes from God, and that is especially true when it comes to the realization that we have some work to do in our walk with him.

In contrast, if you find yourself on the other end of that spectrum, and David's words echo in your heart as well, then praise God, but be sure not to take that relationship for granted. Every day, our love for God can grow or wane based on how we relate to him. And approaching every day committed to seeing it grow is imperative, especially when life makes that choice difficult.

DOUBT DROVE DAVID TO GOD

The third lesson Psalm 27 teaches us on loving God with our affections is that there is room for doubt when times get tough.

David follows up his dramatic prose on all the Lord has done for him and his desire to spend his days in the Lord's presence with an extended plea for God's mercy and protection (vv. 7–12). The abruptness of that shift is somewhat startling, but it's also very true to life. After all, few of us get advance warning that the floor is about to drop out from beneath us. Rather, when the tough times come, they tend to come quickly.

In such moments, it's natural for us to have doubts. We'll talk more about this theme tomorrow, but what's important to notice in this passage is that those questions and fears drive David back to God rather than causing him to pull away from the Lord. And even when it seemed to David like God was pulling away from him, David never wavered in his commitment.

That consistency was possible because David loved the Lord with his affections rather than his emotions. When our relationship with someone is based on how we feel in a given moment, then that relationship will necessarily lack the stability required for any semblance of depth. So it's often in the difficult times when we can see most clearly to what extent our love for God is based in affection rather than emotion.

7. Does your devotion to the Lord tend to vary when times are hard and you encounter the kinds of stress and pain that might make you feel as though he is distant, or do such times drive you closer to him?

DAVID TRUSTED GOD

David concludes Psalm 27 by reiterating the hope and faith he's found in the Lord.

The language he uses, particularly the repeated call to "wait for the Lord," indicates that the difficult times described in the preceding verses have not yet passed in their entirety. Rather, he has chosen to face them with an assurance of God's goodness born of the history they share and his desire to remain in the Lord's presence.

In so doing, he gives us a clear pattern for how to love God with our affections rather than our emotions.

8. Take a few moments to pray and ask God to help you evaluate your relationship with him based on the pattern established in Psalm 27.

9. Which has a greater impact on how you see the Lord today: recent events or the larger history of your relationship with him?

10. When you get ready to pray or open his word to read, are you more excited to start that conversation, or for it to be over so you can go on to something else?

11. How do difficult times impact your walk with the Lord? Do they pull you closer to him or drive you away?

Ultimately, none of us is capable of completely removing the emotional elements of what it means to love, whether with respect to the Lord or to other people. However, we have the choice between allowing those feelings to form the foundation of that relationship or opting instead for the stability born of genuine affection.

When God calls us to love him with all our heart, affection is what he's looking for because he knows that is the best and most reliable way to relate to him. It's also how he relates to us.

12. So, as we conclude for today, take some time to pray and thank God for loving you with affection rather than emotion, and ask for his help in returning that love in kind. Reflect on how you answered the questions throughout today's devotion and ask the Holy Spirit to help you take those thoughts and give them back to the Lord in prayer. Write that prayer down in the space below so you can come back to it in the future as the need arises.

LOVING GOD IN TIMES OF HARDSHIP

NOTE: While these devotionals are largely a collaborative effort, the personal testimony in today's comes from Dr. Ryan Denison.

Over the last few days, we discussed the importance of loving God with our affections rather than our emotions, noting that our affections are more reliable and sustainable than an emotional response.

The importance of that distinction is seen most clearly in the times when the object of our affection is not someone we are particularly fond of at that moment. And while that aspect may seem strange or even out of place when it comes to our love for God, if we're honest with ourselves, then I would imagine all of us have encountered an occasion where our primary feelings toward our heavenly Father were less than positive.

For me, it was shortly after I found out I had cancer.

"I BELIEVE; HELP MY UNBELIEF!"

The initial diagnosis wasn't overly shocking. I'd known that a bump had existed on the side of my neck for several years, but I'd been assured it was nothing to worry about. However, some of the darkest days of my life occurred in the time between finding out that it was cancer and doctors running the necessary tests to determine what type of cancer it was.

That darkness carried over into my relationship with God.

I remember getting out of bed one night, unable to sleep, and making my way into another room because I just needed to vent. In those moments, love was about the last thing I felt toward the Lord. I felt anger, self-pity, and a general sense of frustration that God could have healed me in an instant but, for whatever reason, had chosen not to do so. These feelings overwhelmed any sense of gratitude or fondness that, on some level, I knew I should feel for him.

And to this day I don't think that was wrong.

I do not believe God was offended by my anger or disappointed in my frustrations. I don't think he looked at my pain with any sense of indignation that it was vented in his direction. Rather, I believe he hurt with me, just as any good father feels their child's pain and shares the grief that results from it. He did not reciprocate my anger but simply let me get it all out before responding in a way that made his presence unmistakably real.

When he did, he led me back to one of my favorite passages in Scripture. It's found in Mark 9:14–29, where the father of an epileptic child comes to Jesus and asks Christ if he can heal his son. Jesus responds, "'If you can'! All things are possible for one who believes" (v. 23). The father then immediately cries out, "I believe; help my unbelief!" (v. 24). And Jesus honors that prayer by healing the man's child.

"I believe, help my unbelief!" is, in many ways, my life verse. However, it's rare that I've felt God use it as powerfully as he did in that moment when my unbelief was related less to the questions of "Does God exist?" or "Is Christianity true?" and more to the question of "If God does exist, am I sure I want to have a relationship with him?"

If, in that moment, my love for the Lord was based on my feelings, then our relationship would have been in a very dark place. But it wasn't. I could be disappointed in God, even angry with God, but I could still love God with all my heart because that love was based on something more than how I felt about him in that moment. And the same can be true for every person who has placed their faith in him.

1. Take a moment and think back to a time when you struggled to feel very loving toward the Lord. What event(s) created those feelings? How did you respond?

2. Looking back on it now, what—if anything—would you do differently in your approach to God during those times?

IF, IN THAT MOMENT, MY LOVE FOR THE LORD WAS BASED ON MY *FEELINGS*, THEN OUR RELATIONSHIP WOULD HAVE BEEN IN A VERY DARK PLACE. BUT IT WASN'T. I COULD BE DISAPPOINTED IN GOD, EVEN ANGRY WITH GOD, BUT I COULD STILL *LOVE* GOD WITH ALL MY HEART BECAUSE THAT LOVE WAS BASED ON SOMETHING *MORE* THAN HOW I FELT ABOUT HIM IN THAT MOMENT. AND THE SAME CAN BE TRUE FOR EVERY PERSON WHO HAS PLACED THEIR FAITH IN HIM.

To truly love God with all your heart means to remain committed to him even when you don't like him. It's a choice that we make, one based more on who we know him to be—as a result of both past experience and the testimony of Scripture—than on what we can understand in our times of trouble.

And few people in Scripture demonstrate that balance better than Job.

GOD'S UNCOMFORTABLE REPLY TO JOB

Most people, even many non-Christians, know the basics of Job's story. Few people are associated with pain, struggle, and faithful endurance like Job is, and for good reason.

Job lost everything because God let the accuser send calamities that robbed him of his children, his health, and his fortune, leaving him on the brink of death. (This accuser was not necessarily Satan, despite that being how he is most often referenced.) The only vestiges of Job's previous life that endured were the wife who told him to "curse God and die" (Job 2:9) and a group of friends who just made things worse.

In spite of those circumstances, Job maintained a position that, given the theological understanding of his time, was a complete paradox to his friends. He argued that the torment he suffered was not the result of sin in his life, but that God could still be just and worthy of praise despite his pain.

After spending the better part of thirty-five chapters going back and forth with his would-be comforters on this issue, God then shows up to set the record straight.

It's important to note, however, that when God showed up in that moment, his words were not meant to comfort, and Job's reaction shows little evidence that he felt better about his situation after hearing from the Lord.

Rather, God's response is essentially that he's God and Job is not.

And that kind of stinks.

In Jesus we see that God has the capacity to comfort in ways that no other person can. Even in the Old Testament, the Lord promises to be a comforter to his people in a manner that does not appear to be the case here (Psalm 94:19; Isaiah 51:12).

To be honest, I'm still not really at ease with the way God responds to Job, and I feel like it's one of those passages people tend to let slide without wrestling with that discomfort. I understand the theological necessity of establishing that God is not answerable to us, and I agree with that sentiment. But even after talking with Job, the Lord tells Job's friends that Job was the only one who spoke rightly about him (Job 42:7–8).

3. Take a few moments to reflect on God's interactions with Job. If you're being completely honest with yourself, how do you feel about it? Take the time to ask God why he answered that way, then give him space to respond and write down what, if anything, he shows you.

The answer to that question might not come quickly—or at all—but it's still worth asking, if for no other reason than that it is important for us to feel sufficiently comfortable taking such issues to the Lord. If we find ourselves afraid to ask God why or confront him with our pain when that pain is the driving force in our lives, then we've cut off the necessary paths to receive his comfort.

Empty platitudes, especially when offered to ourselves, won't fix anything. And we can't love God well when we allow our hurts to make us afraid to turn to him.

CHOOSE TO TRUST DESPITE THE PAIN

Ultimately, even though God didn't give Job an answer he could understand, or even one that seemed to give him much comfort in the moment, God still gave him an answer. That appears to have been enough.

It didn't make Job's hurt or his pain go away instantly, and there was likely always part of him that struggled to understand why he'd had to endure what he did. However, the sense of loss never grew stronger than his love for the Lord, so he was able to work through it to embrace God's blessing once again (Job 42:10–17).

In the same way, there will be times when God's answer in the midst of our pain is some variation of: "You can't understand why this is happening." And the truth is that even if we could, oftentimes it wouldn't lessen the burden we feel as a result of those trials.

A key component of loving God with all your heart is making the decision to trust that he is still the good God his word shows him to be, even when our experiences would lead us to question that fact. However, we should not simply ignore the discord that can result in those moments from having to love God on faith rather than feeling.

He can handle our questions, and he is not offended by honest anger. We just need to make sure that, in giving vent to that pain, we never cross the line of forgetting that he is still God and that he may not have what we would deem a good answer for us.

4. So, as we conclude for today, is there some pain in your life that's making it difficult to love God with all your heart? It could be something recent or the residual hurt of a wound that scarred over long ago. Whatever the case may be, start by reminding yourself of who he is as your good, heavenly Father and the love that he has for you. Commit to loving him, even in the midst of the pain. Then take that pain to the Lord and ask him whatever questions come to mind, giving him the necessary space to respond.

5. Write down anything he brings to mind, be it feelings, frustrations, or insights. When you're finished, give yourself some time to breathe and process what he's shown you. And if the sense you were left with is that this was the start of a conversation rather than its conclusion, treat it as such. Then commit to going back to him again in a similar fashion whenever the need should arise.

LOVING GOD BY LEARNING TO BE CONTENT IN HIM

Yesterday, we discussed what it is like to love God even when we don't feel very loving toward him. Making the choice not to let our pain or anger become the primary lens through which we view the Lord is crucial to loving God with all our heart, because such pain is inevitable in this life. Being consistent with that choice is made easier, however, if we can learn to be content in the midst of our circumstances, regardless of what those circumstances may be.

Now, it's important to note that contentment is not synonymous with either apathy or nihilism. Neither choosing not to improve your life nor resigning yourself to accept your circumstances because you think there's no point in making them better are biblical concepts. Far too often, however, we can slip in either direction and mistake the end result for contentment when, really, all we've done is give up.

Loving God with all our heart means actively choosing to prioritize God's will over our own. Any sense of contentment that results will be the product of the peace that comes from placing ourselves entirely in his hands.

Unfortunately, such faith and reliance on the Lord is often far easier said than done. Paul gives us some helpful guidelines, however, on what it should look like.

1. Before we take a closer look at Paul's example, can you think of a time when you loved someone so utterly that being in their presence brought you a sense of peace? What was it about that person and your relationship with them that triggered those feelings?

CHOOSE CONTENTMENT

In Philippians 4, Paul ends his letter by imparting a series of brief lessons on how to live a life of peace and purpose. Some of the most oft-quoted wisdom from his writings occurs in these passages, though the pieces are often taken in isolation from one another rather than viewed within the larger context of the chapter.

Philippians 4:13, for example, is among the most popular verses in the New Testament: "I can do all things through him who strengthens me." However, that idea is often treated as if simply having a relationship with God is some kind of superpower that enables us to get through our trials and persevere in spite of our circumstances. But while there is some truth to that concept, it is a dangerous notion if taken without the context in which the apostle shares that insight in the preceding verses.

Before Paul gets to that popular promise, he writes, "I rejoiced in the Lord greatly that now at length you have revived your concern for me. You were indeed concerned for me, but you had no opportunity. Not that I am speaking of being in need, for I have learned in whatever situation I am to be content. I know how to be brought low, and I know how to abound. In any and every circumstance, I have learned the secret of facing plenty and hunger, abundance and need. I can do all things through him who strengthens me" (Philippians 4:10–13).

Paul can say he can do all things through Christ because he has determined not to let his commitment to the Lord be dependent on his circumstances. His relationship with God is not a parachute that gives him peace because he knows that, if things get really bad, he can just pull the cord and be saved. Rather, his relationship with God is the defining lens through which he views his life, and his love for Jesus is such that he has learned to rely on the Lord's constancy no matter what else is going on around him.

2. When you think about your relationship with the Lord, to what extent do your circumstances dictate how much time you spend with him?

3. How consistent are you in your devotion to God? If you're honest with yourself, how consistent do you really want to be?

Even that contentment, however, is not simply the result of choosing to trust God. Rather, as Paul describes earlier in the chapter, it is a pattern he maintained every day of his life.

HAVE AN ACTIVE FAITH

Starting in verse 4, Paul instructs his readers to "rejoice in the Lord always; again I will say, rejoice. Let your reasonableness be known to everyone. The Lord is at hand; do not be anxious about anything, but in everything by prayer and supplication with thanksgiving let your requests be made known to God. And the peace of God, which surpasses all understanding, will guard your hearts and your minds in Christ Jesus" (Philippians 4:4–7).

He then expounds on that principle by adding, "Finally, brothers, whatever is true, whatever is honorable, whatever is just, whatever is pure, whatever is lovely, whatever is commendable, if there is any excellence, if there is anything worthy of praise, think about these things. What you have learned and received and heard and seen in me— practice these things, and the God of peace will be with you" (Philippians 4:8–9).

Taken together, these passages demonstrate that the reason Paul was able to find contentment regardless of his circumstances is that he had learned to approach every circumstance with rejoicing, prayer, supplication, and thanksgiving.

Moreover, he kept his mind set on the things that foster a closer walk with the Lord rather than on those that are more prone to lead us toward sin and temptation. As a result, he positioned himself to walk every day with "the God of peace" and allow that peace to pervade every facet of his life.

Notice, though, that nothing about what Paul describes is the result of passive acceptance on his part. Everything he writes about in these verses requires us to take an active role in the process. The apostle reminds us that the kind of peace and contentment he describes cannot be found by giving up and simply accepting life as it comes. Rather, it happens when in every circumstance we make the choice to turn to the Lord.

When we are facing plenty, we learn to abound by going to the Lord in thanksgiving and rejoicing in the provision we've received from him. When we face hunger and need, we go to the Lord in prayer and supplication, trusting that he has a plan for us even in times of struggle. And through all of it, we avoid the anxiety that can so easily pull our focus away from him by remembering all he has done for us and setting our minds on what is true, honorable, pure, lovely, commendable, excellent, and worthy of praise.

When we do that, we can know God's peace because we will have learned to abide in his will and rely on him as our source of strength for each day.

4. When you think about the various aspects of what Paul writes in those verses, which part do you find it most difficult to be consistent with?

5. Do you find it easier to turn to God when things are going well or when your circumstances take a more difficult turn? Is your walk with him more consistent in good times or bad?

CONTINUE YOUR COMMITMENT

Contentment plays a key role in loving God with all our heart because it is the result of making the choice to say yes to his will, regardless of our circumstances, and orienting our affections toward him in every facet of our lives. In short, contentment is the product of what we've discussed over the last few days.

The kind of constancy the Lord asks of us does not mean we will never waver in our faith or have moments where loving him is difficult. It does mean, however, that when it gets difficult to love God with all our heart, we will still choose to continue our commitment to him. When we do, we can experience the kind of peace and contentment only he can provide, both of which can make it easier to maintain that love moving forward.

6. Take some time now to ask God to help you find contentment in him. Ask if there are any aspects of your life that make such contentment difficult to achieve. Finally, with those answers in mind, ask the Lord to help you understand the ways in which those issues are making it more difficult for you to love God with all your heart.

7. When you're finished, turn those thoughts into a prayer and write it down as your offering to God.

LOVING YOUR NEIGHBOR WITH YOUR HEART

Over the last five days, we've discussed what it means to love God with all your heart.

- We've looked to Moses and Pharaoh for insight into the importance of saying yes and the consequences of saying no when God asks us to do something.

- We've seen in David a model for loving God with our affections rather than our emotions, noting how the former is more consistent and reliable because it's not based on the whims of how we feel at a given moment.

- We've been reminded by Job of how, if you truly love someone, your circumstances won't diminish that love, even if there are times when God's answers in the midst of our pain may fall short of what we'd hope to receive.

- And last, we've examined Paul's instructions on how to find the Lord's peace and contentment regardless of our circumstances, noting that such contentment is the result of an active choice we must make to pursue God's will above our own.

Yet, when Jesus answered the scribe's question regarding "which commandment is the most important of all" (Mark 12:28), he didn't stop with loving God with our heart, soul, mind, and strength. Rather, he continued by adding—unprompted—that "the second is this: 'You shall love your neighbor as yourself.' There is no other commandment greater than these" (v. 31).

Clearly, as far as Christ is concerned, any conversation about loving God is incomplete unless we include loving our neighbor as well. With that in mind, how should loving God with all our heart inform the way we seek to extend that love to those around us?

For our answer, let's look at a time when Jesus described how he expects his followers to love.

A CALL TO LOVE DESPITE THE COST

1. Take a few moments to read Matthew 25:31–46. Write down any insights that come to mind regarding the kind of love Jesus asks us to show toward others in this passage.

Jesus begins his parable by describing how, when he comes back, he's going to do so in such a way that there can be no doubt he's the Son of God. He'll be in his full heavenly splendor, complete with flocks of angels and a throne from which he'll judge the whole of humanity.

And in that judgment, the standards for salvation will be considerably more than empty words and broken promises to follow his example. Those who have continued his ministry by loving others as he loved them, even though they may not always be the easiest people to love, will be rewarded.

But when did that ever matter to Jesus?

Was it easy to eat with Zacchaeus when Jesus knew that the religious leaders and every other self-respecting Jew would criticize him for it? Was it easy to care for Mary Magdalene and offer her redemption when the rest of society had written her off? Was it easy to pray for those who had driven spikes into his hands and feet before they left to gamble for his clothes?

Jesus chose to love others regardless of what it would cost him or whether they'd done anything to deserve that love. And now he calls us to do the same.

2. Can you think of a time when you have felt a clear call from the Lord to love someone who was difficult to love? Did you follow God's prompting? If so, what was the result?

LOVE IS IN THE PROOF

As with many of Christ's teachings, though, it's not enough to simply know what we are supposed to do. Rather, the emphasis is on understanding and embracing why we should do it, as well.

You see, the righteous in this passage didn't care for those they met in order to get some kind of reward. They were as surprised as anyone else to learn why they were saved. No, they helped the least of these because they knew that's what Jesus would have done. Their actions were the proof of their salvation, not the cause.

Likewise, those who on that day will be condemned to join the devil and his angels were shocked to find that the reason for their condemnation was their failure to serve Christ by serving others. After all, what could be further from the picture of the Son of Man seated on his throne of glory than memories of the beggar they routinely passed by on the street corner or the coworker who ate lunch alone every day? How could this divine figure identify with them?

They didn't get it, and one can't help but wonder if the reason is that they never got close enough to Jesus to look into his merciful, tear-filled eyes whenever he saw someone in need and ask themselves: Why did he do that?

3. Have you ever taken the time to ask those questions? Take a few moments now to do so and write down what insights come to mind.

DESIRE, NOT DUTY

When we read stories about the way Christ cared for people, it can be tempting to assume he did it because it was just in his nature. And there is some truth to that thought. After all, one of the disciples who knew him best would later write that "anyone who does not love does not know God, because God is love" (1 John 4:8).

Still, even though it was in Christ's nature to love, the way he went about doing so is crucial to our present conversation. We've already discussed that it was a choice he made that was not reliant on his circumstances or the degree to which those who received that love deserved it. However, it also seems like his concern went deeper than a simple decision.

Throughout the Gospels, the countenance of Christ drew people in, and that was largely because they understood that his affection for them was genuine. In the same way, our love for those we meet needs to be about more than just checking off another requirement for what we think it means to be a good Christian.

However, such affection can be difficult to muster, at times, which is why it is crucial that it comes as an extension of our affection for God.

It can be strange to think about the love shared between the Father and Son when both are part of the triune God, but Scripture is clear that such love was an integral part of their relationship (John 5:20; 17:24). In the same way, loving God with all our heart is crucial to being able to love others as we love ourselves. And this point is driven home even more clearly in the parable's conclusion.

A READY YES

At this point in Jesus's story, the disciples were likely feeling pretty good about themselves. After all, they'd left behind family, friends, jobs, and security to follow a carpenter from Galilee while he changed the world. If salvation were as simple as making the most of the time and resources God has given us, they'd done that.

And I'm sure Jesus was very pleased that they'd chosen to follow him. They really were making the most of their time by being with him. But he knew that in a few days he'd be leaving them to return to the Father in heaven and they'd have to follow him in a different way—and it wouldn't be easy.

So he gave them this one final truth to tie together all that they'd witnessed and heard over the last three years, even if they wouldn't quite understand it until they saw him arrested, naked, thirsty, hungry, and alone up on that cross.

You see, Jesus did identify with the least of these in a very real way, and he still has the scars to prove it.

Christ's message in this parable can be hard to understand and even harder to follow. It requires more of us than we're often willing to give. But perhaps the reason is that we look at it from the perspective of fallen humanity trying to serve fallen humanity instead of the redeemed Christ serving those for whom he came to die.

The righteous in the story didn't know that they were helping Christ, but I think they knew they were continuing his work. Jesus doesn't expect us to be able to help every homeless person we meet or have the right answer for everyone who is struggling, but he does expect us to be willing to be his hands and feet to a world that needs to understand his love and see it in us.

So, when he calls us to love others as we love ourselves, we need to be ready to say yes rather than harden our hearts against his will. And make no mistake: That call is a yes-or-no question every time we receive it.

Making the right choice gets easier, however, when our hearts are fully aligned with God's. After all, loving others will not always be as straightforward as giving them a meal or sitting with them in a time of need. As we discussed on day 4, such sacrifices must be made in accordance with the Holy Spirit's guidance, and that guidance is much easier to follow when we are walking closely with the Lord.

Ultimately, God has put the least of these in all of our lives not only for their sake but also for ours. And extending our love for God to our love for others draws us closer to both.

SO WHEN HE CALLS US TO *LOVE OTHERS* AS WE LOVE
OURSELVES, WE NEED TO BE READY TO SAY *YES* RATHER
THAN HARDEN OUR HEARTS AGAINST HIS WILL.
AND MAKE NO MISTAKE: THAT CALL IS A YES-OR-NO
QUESTION *EVERY* TIME WE RECEIVE IT.

4. So, as we conclude for today, take some time to ask the Lord to give you an honest evaluation of the degree to which your love for him has extended to your love for others. Pray for examples of where you've done that well, and also examples of where you've fallen short.

5. When you're finished, take those thoughts and form them into a prayer, asking the Lord to help you approach each day with a heightened awareness of the opportunities he brings you to extend your love for him to others.

HOW TO LOVE GOD WITH ALL YOUR SOUL

In Greek and Hebrew thought, the soul served a similar purpose to how many see the heart today. As we discussed in the previous section, the biblical view of the heart portrayed it more as the seat of decisions rather than of our passions and emotions, with the soul filling that latter role.

As such, loving God with your soul carries with it the idea of personal devotion and spiritual growth in a way that centers our lives on our relationship with God.

In this section we'll look at the ways in which we can better learn to love God by developing our personal walk with him. That effort has to start, however, with making sure that we've recognized him as our king.

One of the primary impediments to loving God well is treating him as if he is something less than the absolute, divine ruler of all creation. Yes, he is our heavenly Father, and yes he longs to have a personal, intimate relationship with us. But we must not cross that line of growing so comfortable with God that we take him for granted or forget what an honor it truly is to have that kind of relationship.

And one of the best ways to maintain that balance is by spending time with him in prayer.

It's through prayer that we open ourselves up to the Holy Spirit's guidance and the intimate connection that can foster true understanding of both who God is and who we are by comparison. But true prayer is more than just talking into the void and assuming that the Lord is listening. It's meant to be a connection between our soul and his Spirit. It's an honest line of communication that goes both ways.

And as a result, it's also a form of worship, which stands as another means of loving God with our soul.

In true worship, we humble ourselves before God, praising him for who he is and what he's done. It's important to note, however, that the form of that worship can be as unique as the person offering it. If we're not careful, we can fall into the trap of attempting to conform our praise of God to the examples we see from those around us. It's great to worship alongside other believers, but we must never forget that, even then, it's ultimately about our soul connecting to the Lord.

One of the best ways to foster that connection is through the spiritual disciplines.

While we won't go into great depth on the spiritual disciplines in these devotionals, a basic understanding of and appreciation for the ways in which they can help us create good habits and patterns in our walk with the Lord can help us learn to love God with our soul more consistently.

As that conversation concludes, we'll turn once again to how loving God with your soul can help you better love your neighbor as yourself. While we should never elevate other people to the place of worship or lordship that God is due, understanding the importance of forming genuine connections with people that extend beyond the transactional relationships that are far more common is crucial to loving others as the Lord intends.

So, as we get ready to learn more about what it means to love God with your soul, let's pause for today and turn to God in prayer.

1. Ask God to help you understand what preconceived notions you have about prayer. How often are you genuinely connecting with the Lord when you pray?

2. When you think about singing songs to God—in church, at home, in the car, etc.—what motivates that worship? Are you singing because you like the song, or because it connects your soul with the Lord? There's a place for both, but giving thought to what drives your worship can provide a helpful perspective for understanding how well you're worshiping God with all your soul.

3. Finally, take those thoughts and turn them into a prayer to the Lord. Write it down in the space below.

MAKING GOD YOUR KING

In Greek and Hebrew thought, the soul served a similar purpose to how many see the heart today. As we discussed in the previous section, the biblical view of the heart portrayed it more as the seat of decisions rather than of our passions and emotions, with the soul filling that latter role. So loving God with your soul carries with it the idea of personal devotion and spiritual growth in a way that centers our lives on our relationship with God.

To that end, over the coming days we will examine how we can better learn to love God by developing our personal walk with him. That effort has to start, however, with making sure we've recognized him as our king.

1. Before we go further, take a few moments to reflect on how you see God. Which of his characteristics stands out most prominently in your mind? When you go to God in prayer, how do you prefer to think about him?

GOD IS NOT A HOBBY

One of the primary impediments to loving God well is treating him as if he's something less than the absolute, divine ruler of all creation. That's not to minimize the equally true reality that he is also our heavenly Father. Nor is it meant to create a degree of separation between us and him. After all, Jesus died to make sure such a chasm would not exist and to enable us to enter into a personal, intimate relationship with the Lord.

However, we must never grow so comfortable with God that we take him for granted or lose sight of what an honor it is to have that kind of relationship. Unfortunately, relating to God as our king has grown increasingly difficult in a culture that often prefers to treat him as a hobby.

In the West, we often separate the soul from the body, the spiritual from the secular, and leave God in our chapels and churches. Christianity is for church, religion is for Sunday, and that's where its relevance stops.

And what is more tragic still is the degree to which his people have bought into that error as well.

You see, God can only lead those who are willing to follow, and he can only bless those who will receive his gifts. He has a good, pleasing, and perfect will for us, a plan to prosper us and not to harm us, to give us hope and a future (Jeremiah 29:11 NIV). But he can only do that when he is our king.

2. When you consider what it means for someone to be a king, what qualities come to mind? Is your general view of what that means positive or negative?

3. In what ways might those preconceived notions impact the way you view God as king?

In biblical times, the idea of a king was a powerful and relevant image. Today, it can be easy to think of it as either a ceremonial vestige from a bygone era or like the despotic tyrants who litter our history books. And while I think most Christians understand that God is neither, rightly rejecting those misconceptions should not include ignoring the concept of what it means for him to be our king altogether.

THE PROBLEM WITH CROWNING A KING

For better or worse, kings in the biblical era were typically charged with setting the direction for the culture within their realm. That's why throughout much of the Old Testament we see God's people prosper under rulers who are committed to him and fall to ruin when their leaders begin to stray. And God knew that would be the case. It's why his original intent was to be Israel's king and why Samuel was so reluctant to ordain a human to take God's place (1 Samuel 8).

History shows that Samuel was right to be wary, yet something in fallen humanity bristles at the notion of a king we can't see, of entrusting our guidance to God. That's been the case since the Garden of Eden, and we'd be foolish to think it's something we've moved beyond today. But just because we may not like the idea of being under a king's reign does not lessen our need for one.

After all, the fact remains that most people want there to be a king . . . so long as it's them.

Therein lies our problem, and one of the greatest impediments to loving the Lord well.

God does not cease to be our king when we try to live as though he's not. As a result, any attempts to fill that role ourselves—or place another person atop that throne— lead to a civil war in our soul. When we fight against the notion of allowing God to be the absolute ruler of our lives and to set the direction for every facet of our being, then we are fighting against the very nature of what he's trying to accomplish in our lives.

4. Can you think of a time when you warred against God in this way? What kind of collateral damage did it cause in your relationship with him and your relationships with other people?

5. If you are currently fighting that battle, what is keeping you from surrendering to the Lord and placing your life in his hands?

Our default position is to try to sit on the throne of our lives. That's why we have to make the conscious decision to make God our king every day. Jesus called it taking up your cross, and he promised that "whoever would save his life will lose it, but whoever loses his life for my sake will find it" (Matthew 16:25).

To worship God with all our soul, we have to let go of the desire for control that would make petty tyrants of us all and, instead, surrender that throne back to God, our perfect and holy King.

THE MISTAKE WE CAN'T MAKE

Ultimately, our love is hollow if the object of our affection is a fictionalized representation rather than the real person. When we portray God as anything less than the king of all creation, then we are worshiping a false god.

That is not a mistake we can afford to make if we want to have a close, personal relationship with the Lord.

6. So, as we conclude for today, look back over the answers you gave to the previous questions. Ask God to forgive you for the ways in which you've attempted to make him something less than your king. Be as specific as memory will allow.

7. When you're done, ask the Holy Spirit to convict you of any ways you're currently attempting to keep his throne for yourself and of any attempts to do so in the future.

8. Last, turn those thoughts into a final prayer in which you surrender the role of king of your life back to God and write that prayer down in the space below.

PRAYER

Yesterday, we discussed the importance of recognizing God as our king and embracing that concept as the first step to loving him with all our soul. The reason was that we cannot love the Lord well or have an intimate relationship with him if the object of our affection is more a false god of our own design than the true God of the Bible.

That distinction is equally relevant to our topic for today: engaging with God in prayer.

One of the best ways to maintain the proper balance between loving God as our heavenly Father and respecting him as the supreme King of all creation is by spending time in his presence. It's through prayer that we can foster a true understanding of both who God is and who we are by comparison.

True prayer, however, is more than just talking into the void and assuming that the Lord is listening. It's meant to be a connection between our soul and his Spirit, an honest line of communication that goes in both directions.

1. Before we continue, take a few moments to reflect on your communication with God.

ONE OF THE *BEST* WAYS TO MAINTAIN THE PROPER
BALANCE BETWEEN LOVING GOD AS OUR HEAVENLY
FATHER AND RESPECTING HIM AS THE SUPREME KING OF
ALL CREATION IS BY SPENDING *TIME* IN HIS PRESENCE.

2. When you pray, how closely does it resemble the kind of conversation you would have with your spouse or a best friend? How closely do you think it should?

3. When you pray, do you expect God to answer, or is it more something you do because you know you're supposed to?

We'll address those issues and more in the rest of today's devotion, but being aware of the biases and tendencies we bring into these discussions is important to gaining an honest understanding of what our relationship with God should look like. And that is particularly the case when it comes to prayer, a concept that many are familiar with but which few give much deep thought.

THE PROBLEM OF PRAYER

Many people struggle to maintain a consistent life of prayer because the concept of prayer is confusing.

Does my prayer convince God to do something he would not otherwise do? If so, then am I talking God into doing the right thing? Am I better than him and must convince him to do what is right?

On the other hand, if my prayer does not change God and his work, then why pray?

I know that some say, "Prayer doesn't change God; prayer changes me." That's true to an extent, but what do we do when we're not the ones who need changing? What about a child in need of healing? A lost person in need of saving? Or a country in need of transformation?

In short, if I pray, do I convince God to do something good? If I don't, then why should I pray?

Do you see the problem?

I would love to give you a clear, concise, and still theologically correct answer to those questions. Unfortunately, I don't think one exists.

As with many paradoxes of the faith, to the extent that an answer is clear and concise, it usually falls short of being correct. Conversely, the most accurate answers often prove difficult to articulate well and, even when they are well articulated, still do not provide complete certainty.

Still, the truth is that we don't have to fully understand prayer in order to pray, and Scripture gives us some clear guidelines to help us communicate with God well.

WHEN THE DOOR DOESN'T OPEN

One of the most important passages on prayer is found in the Sermon on the Mount. In Matthew 7, Jesus gave his disciples a series of commands: "Ask and it will be given to you; seek, and you will find; knock, and it will be opened to you" (Matthew 7:7).

Those commands were followed with a series of promises: "Everyone who asks receives, and the one who seeks finds, and to the one who knocks it will be opened" (v. 8).

But has that been your experience?

I can think of many times when it feels like I asked and was ignored, that I sought God and found nothing, and that I knocked on a door that appeared to remain shut. Chances are, you can as well.

So how do we reconcile that experience with the promises of Jesus?

Some would argue that when the Lord does not appear to answer, it's because we did not ask with sufficient faith. However, Jesus told his disciples that they could move mountains with faith the size of a mustard seed and honored a father's request to "help my unbelief" (Matthew 17:20; Mark 9:24).

Is some measure of faith necessary to relate properly to the Lord? Absolutely. But does he refuse to bless us because we fail to meet some arbitrary and unknown standard of belief? That idea is both unbiblical and contrary to the heavenly Father that Jesus described in this passage.

As he said in the very next verses, "Which one of you, if his son asks him for bread, will give him a stone? Or if he asks for a fish, will give him a serpent? If you then, who are evil, know how to give good gifts to your children, how much more will your Father who is in heaven give good things to those who ask him!" (Matthew 7:9–11).

Bread in ancient Israel often bore a close resemblance to the sun-parched stones one would encounter on the roads that traversed the country. In fact, many of those in attendance had likely passed by such stones on their way to hear Jesus. Likewise, snakes were commonly found among the fish and eels caught in the lakes of first-century Judea, but were considered unclean to eat.

In both examples, the idea is that no good father would trick his child into trying to eat something that was bad for them. The pagan gods that Jesus warned us not to confuse with the one true God might have done such a thing, but our heavenly Father would not.

But, again, has that always been your experience with God? If not, why not?

4. Before we return to God's word for guidance on those questions, take some time to really wrestle with the degree to which your experiences with prayer have seemed to measure up to what Jesus described in this passage. Are there any lingering areas of hurt or disappointment from your past that might be impacting your prayers today?

THE DIFFERENCE BETWEEN GIFTS AND GOOD GIFTS

By this point in the sermon, Jesus had established that God is both aware of our needs and more than capable of meeting them. However, he had also made clear that he will only do so when we trust him enough to accept his provision, even when it may not be what we were hoping to receive.

Going back to the rocks and snakes, to a hungry child riding down the road or sitting by the sea in ancient Israel, it's easy to imagine a rock or snake looking quite tasty to their naive eyes. It's also easy to imagine such a child becoming incensed when their father refused to give them what they were so certain they wanted.

When we allow our anxieties and worries to make us doubt the faithfulness of our heavenly Father, it can be easy to become that petulant child. We feel the rumble in our stomachs, see what appears to be an appetizing answer, and cannot understand why God would refuse to grant our request.

But if we look back again at the end of verse 11, Jesus did not promise that our heavenly Father will give us the gifts for which we ask. Rather, he promised to give us *good* gifts when we ask.

This side of heaven, we may not always understand how God's answers to our prayers could be considered good. However, he has given us more than enough evidence to trust that they are. And such trust is built through open, honest, and consistent communication with him.

As we discussed when we looked at Job's love for the Lord, God's not afraid of our doubts, anger, or frustrations. We can take those emotions too far if they get in the way of our seeing God's love, justice, and holiness as his primary attributes, but we don't have to hide those things when we pray. God is not fooled by any facade we can muster, and ignoring the issues that stand between you and him will just drive you further from the only one who can truly help you heal.

HOW TO HAVE A MORE CONSISTENT PRAYER LIFE

While the nature of our conversation on prayer has, to this point, tended toward addressing the issues that can make conversing with the Lord more challenging, we'd be remiss if we did not take a moment to discuss some practical ways to make that conversation easier.

The best way to improve the ease with which we can talk to God in prayer is to simply pray more often.

After all, when Paul writes that we are to "pray without ceasing" (1 Thessalonians 5:17), he was not using hyperbole. That doesn't mean that our every waking moment should be spent in prayer, but that we should just do our best never to close those lines of communication.

To that end, one tip that has proved beneficial is to avoid saying *amen* unless the prayer is public.

If you grew up in the church or learned to pray primarily in a communal setting, chances are that the part of your soul engaged in communing with the Lord tends to shut down when amen is uttered. It's kind of like a period at the end of the sentence or the final credits after a movie.

Oftentimes, not saying amen when the prayer is just between you and God can be a helpful way of remembering that, even if you're done talking, you should not be done listening. It's a way to keep those lines of communication open so that when the Holy Spirit chooses to speak, you're better positioned to hear him.

A second tip is to pray about everything.

Chances are, which parking spot you take or which gallon of milk you choose at the store is not a decision that bears eternal significance. However, taking the time to ask the Lord to guide even our smallest and seemingly most insignificant decisions makes it easier to recognize his voice when the big decisions come.

The two suggestions given above are by no means an exhaustive list, and they may seem a bit trivial on the surface. However, anything that gets us talking to God more often will improve our prayer life and, by extension, our relationship with the Lord. So, with that in mind, let's finish our time for today by going to God in prayer.

5. Take a few moments to look back over the answers you gave to the earlier questions in today's devotion. In light of those answers, be honest with God and address any issues he has brought to mind.

6. When you're done, spend the next few minutes in silence. Write down anything he shows you and whatever feelings come up as you listen. If you're not used to it, a few minutes of silence may seem like a really long time, but do your best not to check your watch or phone.

7. Last, go back to God with what he's shown you. Ask for this to be the start of a conversation rather than its end. Write your prayer down so you can revisit it as needed (just remember not to say amen).

ADDITIONAL RESOURCES

- To delve deeper into the big questions surrounding prayer, request *The Greater Work: How Prayer Positions You to Receive All that Grace Intends to Give* by Dr. Jim Denison.

- For biblically based guided prayers, request *Every Hour I Need Thee: A Practical Guide to Daily Prayer* by Dr. Jim Denison.

WORSHIP

Yesterday, we discussed the importance of being honest with God and that prayer was meant to be a link between our soul and God's Spirit. When that happens, our prayers become a form of worship in that they offer a direct avenue of connection between us and the Lord. And that connection resides at the heart of what it means to worship God well, regardless of the form of that worship.

You see, worship is about more than just singing praises to the Lord. The form it takes can be as unique as the person who offers it. If we're not careful, though, we can fall into the trap of attempting to conform the praise we offer to the examples we see from others around us.

While it's great to worship alongside other believers, we must never forget that, even then, it's ultimately about our soul connecting with God. Learning how to do that well will be our focus for today.

1. When you think of worship, what comes to mind first?

2. What are some examples of the ways people worship something other than God? Is there anything in your life besides the Lord that vies for your worship?

WORSHIP IS MORE THAN MUSIC

Terry York, one of my (Ryan's) professors in seminary, changed the way I see worship quite a bit during my time in his class. One of the most significant things was the way he emphasized that worship is about more than just the music. When we discussed planning a service, he wanted us to see the preaching, communion, offering, and even the time spent greeting others that morning, as acts of worship as well.

And he was right to do so.

Whether it's corporate worship in a church, sitting alone in a quiet room, or something in between, worship is about connecting with God in honest praise and adoration of who he is, thereby positioning ourselves to hear from him and relate to him in whatever way he chooses to respond.

For some—perhaps most—that goal can best be accomplished through music. After all, if you've ever found yourself singing along to an old song you haven't heard for years, then you can understand a bit about why music can be a powerful way to worship the Lord.

Truths sung have a way of sticking with us in a way that those heard may not. And even in private times of worship, music can help us connect our souls with God's Spirit. Yet, not everyone worships best through music, and that's all right as well.

Personally, I've always connected with God more easily through sermons and time spent in contemplation. That tendency is likely due, at least in part, to the fact that I have an awful voice and that it takes a great deal of faith for me to believe I'm capable of producing anything that even my heavenly Father would consider a joyful noise. As such, I tend to get self-conscious during the times of music, which makes it difficult to fully engage with the Lord through that medium. In the same way, my introverted nature makes getting out of my chair to talk with people prior to the service difficult as well.

Fortunately, God knows how I'm wired because he's the one who made me. And the same is true for you as well.

3. Before we continue, take some time to reflect and ask the Lord to help you understand in what ways you connect with him best. How can those forms of connection inform how you approach worshiping him?

4. Are there any ways in which your views of worship have been too narrow?

GOD DOES NOT HAVE A PREFERENCE FOR THE *FORM*
OF OUR WORSHIP SO LONG AS IT IS *HONEST* IN NATURE
AND KEEPS OUR FOCUS ON *CONNECTING* WITH HIM.

God does not have a preference for the form of our worship so long as it is honest in nature and keeps our focus on connecting with him. However, just because you may engage with the Lord best through one avenue of worship doesn't mean that the others aren't important as well. And when we start to limit the means by which we can connect with him to what feels most natural to us, we also limit the means by which he can connect with us.

If we want to worship God well, then we need to remember that he is not just the object of our worship but also the one who gets to direct it.

WHAT TRUE WORSHIP REQUIRES

Throughout Scripture, one issue that upsets God the most is when his people try to use worship as a means to their ends. And while that can start in any number of ways, the tendency often goes back to the temptation to approach worship from the perspective that it's a gift God should be grateful to receive rather than an expression of our gratitude to the Lord.

And if you ever had any doubt about that fact, Isaiah 1 should put the matter to rest.

5. Before we continue, take a moment to read Isaiah 1:10–20.

In this passage, God started by calling the leaders of his people to listen before describing how every element of their worship—from their sacrifices to their feasts and prayers—amounted to nothing more than "vain offerings" (v. 13) and had become "a burden to me" (v. 14) because of the hearts with which they were offered.

To make matters worse, the people had become so accustomed to this empty and perfunctory worship that they appear to have had no idea that what they were doing was wrong. After all, their laws—written by God, no less—mandated that they do all these things, so they were being obedient in their worship. Why was the Lord so upset?

He answered that question starting in verse 16: "Wash yourselves; make yourselves clean; remove the evil of your deeds from before my eyes; cease to do evil, learn to do good; seek justice, correct oppression; bring justice to the fatherless, plead the widow's cause" (Isaiah 1:16–17).

In short, their worship appeared from the outside to be righteous. However, the time and resources sacrificed at the altar represented the entirety of what they were willing to give God. Every other facet of their lives remained within their control and was seen as irrelevant to the Lord. So, God had no bearing on how they lived.

God did not create us to have that kind of transactional relationship with him.

It was, however, how every other religion of their time thought the relationship between people and their gods was supposed to work. Unfortunately, that's still the case far too often in our culture today.

The notion that worship on a Sunday morning is enough to make God happy and grant me his favor for the rest of the week remains a perverse yet pervasive distortion of what the Lord wants from us in worship. However, when we are the ones who decide what that worship should look like, that's what it will often entail.

So, as we conclude for today, it's vital for us to understand that true worship—worship that leads us to love God with all our soul—must retain God as its focus and its author. He is the one who gets to decide how we will worship him. And while that may look different for you than it does for me, we can know that it will include presenting every facet of our lives "as a living sacrifice, holy and acceptable to God, which is your spiritual worship" (Romans 12:1).

6. With that basic truth in mind, take some time now to pray, and ask God to reveal any areas of your life that you've deemed off-limits to him. To put it another way, is there any part of your life that could not be presented to God as a living sacrifice? If so, ask the Spirit to reveal the ways in which that sin is impeding your worship of the Lord.

7. When you're done, take those thoughts and turn them into a prayer. Make that prayer part of your worship of God today.

SPIRITUAL DISCIPLINES

Over the last four days, we've discussed the importance of making God your king and then engaging with him through prayer and worship. One theme through each of those days is the need to be sure that we don't allow false preconceptions of who God is, or who we are in relation to him, to get in the way of an open and thriving walk with the Lord. Spending consistent time with God is key to ensuring we avoid such a mistake.

However, such consistency requires discipline. The spiritual disciplines can be one of the most effective means of fostering a healthy relationship with the Lord.

While we won't go into great depth on any of the individual disciplines today,[1] a basic understanding of and appreciation for the ways in which these disciplines aid us in creating good habits and patterns in our walk with the Lord can help us learn to love God with our soul more consistently.

Before we go further, though, it's important to state from the start that the spiritual disciplines are meant to be a means to the end of a closer walk with the Lord. They are tools we place in the Holy Spirit's hands to use as he sees fit, but they must never replace God as the focus of our time and efforts.

---

1   For a more detailed treatment of the subject of spiritual disciplines, see "What does the Bible say about spiritual health?" at DenisonForum.org.

1. Now, take a few moments to reflect on any preconceived notions or experiences you may have regarding the idea of spiritual disciplines. What thoughts first come to mind? Are they primarily positive, negative, or neutral?

2. When you think about engaging in a spiritual discipline, how do you feel?

While there are a number of ways to discuss spiritual disciplines, for the purposes of today's devotion we will group them into two categories: vertical and horizontal. Our hope is that by organizing them in this fashion, we can see how they work together to guide us to a closer walk with the Lord in every facet of our lives.

VERTICAL DISCIPLINES

Vertical disciplines help us maintain a healthy spiritual life with God. They include meditation, solitude, and fasting.

MEDITATION

Meditation is an active discipline, not a passive one. It connects you to the living God and his purpose for you.

It can be tempting to regard meditation as an Eastern concept—and one that has little place in Christianity—but that would be a mistake. The Eastern form generally calls upon the practitioner to empty self and become nothing. In contrast, Christian meditation calls those who practice it to be filled and transformed.

Through meditation, we can stay better equipped—spiritually and emotionally—to face the trials and temptations of life. When you listen to God's voice, you can respond in obedience to his word. The world constantly pulls us in multiple directions. Meditation allows a person to focus on what is important.

So, how does a Christian meditate?

It's like learning to ride a bike. You don't really know how, no matter how much you've studied, until you climb on and experience it. Basically, you learn to meditate by meditating.

Start by choosing something through which God has often spoken to you. For example, it could be a favorite passage of Scripture, getting out in nature, or a favorite song of worship. Then spend time in prayer and contemplation, asking the Lord to reveal himself and speak to you through that medium.

It may sound mystical, but it's really just about letting go of your thoughts and giving the Holy Spirit the freedom to direct them as he sees fit. Such open and honest communication will draw you closer to the Lord in a way that can be difficult in our culture today, which leads to the second vertical discipline.

SOLITUDE

The fear of being alone drives some of us to constant noise. But we must not mistake being alone with feeling lonely. Loneliness is inner emptiness; solitude is inner fulfillment.

Besides, solitude is not about being alone; it's about being focused. When our times of solitude are directed toward an intentional interaction with the Lord, we're the furthest thing from being alone.

And if you're ever tempted to think you don't need that time away from others, remember that even Jesus found it necessary to be alone with his Father. He needed that time of solitude and focus for leadership and direction in his life. If Jesus needed the discipline of solitude, how much more do we?

So what are some ways we can practice solitude more regularly?

For starters, set aside a time each day to simply be alone with the Lord, and be vigilant in protecting it. Treat it like you would a date with your spouse or dinner with your closest friend. Make it a vital and uncompromising part of your day. Your time of solitude doesn't have to be long, but the more consistent you can be in setting it aside, the more productive it will prove to be.

Then take advantage of the small bits of time that pop up throughout your day. Stuck in traffic or waiting for an appointment? Spend some time in prayer, listen to the Bible, or turn on a Christian podcast. Our days are filled with short, relatively insignificant intervals that can add up to substantial improvement in our walk with the Lord if we use them to draw closer to him.

Then, where you can, try to set aside longer periods to get away and just be with God. It could be an annual prayer retreat, a weekend every few months, or even just a day of vacation that's spent with God instead of other people. But getting extended time to focus on your walk with the Lord can make an enormous difference in your relationship with him.

FASTING

The third vertical discipline is fasting.

Throughout the Bible, fasting is typically defined as abstaining from food for spiritual purposes. Sometimes it's meant to help people focus on prayer. At other times it's done to beseech God's help or as a sign of repentance.

Regardless of the purpose, though, fasting is simply taking time that you would normally spend on yourself and redirecting it to your relationship with God.

That can be done by giving up something other than food. Fasting from social media, electronics, or anything else that normally takes up a good amount of your free time and thinking can be just as helpful as fasting from food. Let God be the one to decide in what ways you will fast, and then commit to obeying his prompting.

However, that is often easier said than done. Because fasting is a foreign concept to many Christians today, it can be difficult to know where to start or how to make the most of that extra time.

The first thing to keep in mind is that, when you fast, you don't have to share that fact with everyone you meet. Jesus was quite clear that anyone who fasts in order to gain recognition from others will gain little else as a result (Matthew 6:16–18). If you feel like you need help or accountability to maintain the fast, then that's different, but be vigilant to ensure that your motivations for fasting don't stray from a focus on God.

Next, once you've committed to fasting, remember to make the Lord part of the conversation when it comes to how you will go about it. Partial fasts can be just as effective as full fasts if the time is used according to the Spirit's guidance. You don't have to fast all day or abstain from everything you enjoy if that's not something God has asked you to do. So, learn to trust the Lord's direction and allow him to be the one who sets the guardrails for your fast before it starts.

3. Before we move on to the horizontal disciplines, take a few moments to reflect on the vertical disciplines we just discussed. Which of those three comes most naturally to you?

4. Is there one that always seems to represent a struggle? Ask God to help you understand why that's the case and write down what he shows you.

HORIZONTAL DISCIPLINES

The horizontal disciplines—Bible study, accountability, and confession—are meant to help us engage with God by engaging with other people. We need people in our lives who see us the way God does and who see the world around us differently than we do. While your relationship with the Lord is personal, it is not meant to be lived in isolation.

With that perspective in mind, let's begin with a look at Bible study.

BIBLE STUDY

Bible study is among the disciplines that can yield the greatest changes in a believer's spiritual life. By itself, church attendance doesn't change us. Serving on committees won't either. Singing in the choir, or even reading the Bible, won't have all that dramatic of an impact either.

But a deep embrace of God's word will. Jesus said, "You will know the truth, and the truth will set you free" (John 8:32).

The discipline of Bible study leads you to experience what you have read.

- First, one learns what the Scripture says.
- Next is applying and obeying it. It moves from your head to your heart.
- Finally, you continue in God's word, applying it to your lifestyle.

His word is the only food God provides for the soul. Nothing else works.

And while we do not need anyone but God to help us understand his word, there is something special about getting together with other people to study Scripture. The different perspectives that emerge from combining the insights given by the Holy Spirit to those in attendance can make for a richer, deeper understanding of the Bible.

So, while private study is important, do not neglect or underestimate the importance of studying God's word with others as well.

ACCOUNTABILITY

Scripture tells us that we are all accountable to God (2 Corinthians 5:10; Romans 14:12). But we are also to hold each other accountable. In Luke 17:3, Jesus says, "If your brother sins, rebuke him, and if he repents, forgive him."

Our burdens are too great for us to carry alone. God never intended Christianity to be a solo act. We are to bear one another's burdens (Galatians 6:2). We need each other.

However, finding open and honest accountability with someone whose views and critiques you can accept can be difficult. It requires a level of mutual trust and devotion to the Lord that takes time to develop. It's worth the cost, though, and if you wait to try to develop those relationships until your sin makes you keenly aware of your need for them, then you're setting yourself up to fail.

So, start by asking God to help you recognize who in your life you trust enough to fill that need. If no one comes to mind, ask the Lord to bring you such a friend.

All of us need accountability, but of the spiritual disciplines, it's perhaps the most uncomfortable to practice.

CONFESSION

All the horizontal disciplines relate to how we treat others and how we are perceived by them. These disciplines aim at transforming our minds to conform us to the image of Christ (Romans 8:28–29). In the process, they bring to the surface old habits, entrenched sin, and bad attitudes that need changing. And we are not really transformed until these changes occur.

God is a God of redemption and forgiveness. When Jesus died on the cross, he took upon himself the sin of the world. God "made him to be sin who knew no sin" (2 Corinthians 5:21). This was the only way total redemption was possible. The Bible promises, "If we confess our sins, he is faithful and just to forgive us our sins and to cleanse us from all unrighteousness" (1 John 1:9). As such, confession is really only a threat to our pride, since we need not fear God's judgment.

The first step to engaging well with the discipline of confession is to admit that we need it. Agree with God and call sin what it is: sin. Then, once you've confessed it, embrace the forgiveness that only Christ can provide, and leave that sin behind. After all, such turning from our sins and temptations is what it means to repent, and repentance is essential to a strong walk with the Lord.

5. Before we conclude for today, take some time to ask God once again to point out which of these disciplines come most naturally to you and which need the most work. What factors make it difficult to put in the work when we know there is an aspect of our relationship with God that is deficient?

6. Take those answers and turn them into a prayer, asking the Lord to help you engage with both the vertical and horizontal disciplines more consistently. Write your prayer down.

DAY 18

LOVING YOUR NEIGHBOR WITH YOUR SOUL

As with our study of what it means to love God with your heart, we're going to conclude our discussion of what it means to love God with your soul by taking those days' devotionals and applying them to the second of the commandments Jesus highlighted: loving your neighbor as yourself.

Remember, our love for others is meant to flow out of our love for the Lord. So loving God well should invariably equip us to love our neighbor well also.

We should never elevate other people to the place of worship or lordship that God is due. However, understanding the importance of forming genuine connections with people that extend beyond the transactional relationships that are far more common is crucial to loving our neighbor as the Lord intends.

1. To that end, begin by looking back over your notes from the previous five days. What stands out most to you about what was discussed? Is there one aspect of what it means to love God with your soul that proves particularly challenging for you? Is there an area that comes most naturally?

With those thoughts in mind, let's shift our focus to how we can apply those lessons to loving others.

RECOGNIZE YOUR RELATIONAL REALITIES

While many aspects of loving God with your soul pertain to loving your neighbor as yourself, the one that applies most directly is the need to relate to who the other person really is rather than who we might wish them to be. And this need is often felt most acutely at the extremes of our relationships.

Whether it's with your children, your spouse, or even a best friend, it can be easy at times to overlook a person's flaws or rationalize away the negatives of their character and the way they act at times. That's not to say we should focus on the negative, but recognizing that all of us are flawed and avoiding the temptation to place them on a pedestal is crucial for loving them well.

As we discussed in day five, a key component of biblical love is the willingness to hold others accountable for the ways in which they have strayed from God's will for their lives. But generally speaking, those are not fun conversations, and it's understandable if you might be hesitant to engage with the people closest to you in a way that might hurt their feelings or cause a potential rift in that relationship.

Yet, if we allow our love for another person to blind us to their faults, then we are not doing our part to help them grow in their relationship with the Lord.

If, on the other hand, our love for them is based in our love for God, then it will be more difficult to ignore their sin when we are walking closely with our holy heavenly Father.

Conversely, when it comes to loving our enemies—something Christ was clear that we are called to do (Matthew 5:43–48)—it can be easy to see only their faults and flaws while ignoring any good that is present within them. This too is a mistake born of the inability to take an honest assessment of who they are and then relate to them in the context of that more accurate understanding.

While there are individuals in this world who are genuinely and thoroughly evil, most of the people we meet are more like us than we might care to admit: a combination of good and bad that, while it may lean more strongly in one direction than the other, is ultimately somewhere in the middle. But if you don't like someone—and especially when things get so bad that you don't *want* to like someone—acknowledging the good in them is difficult.

THE CLOSER WE GET TO GOD, THE MORE WE ARE INCLINED TO SEE *THE WORLD AS HE DOES*, AND THAT INCLUDES HOW HE SEES OTHER PEOPLE. THE LORD IS FAR FROM IGNORANT OF OUR FAULTS, YET HE CHOOSES TO *LOVE US* IN SPITE OF THEM. THERE IS NO AMOUNT OF SIN THAT CAN PREVENT HIM FROM SEEING THE PART OF US THAT REMAINS CREATED *IN HIS IMAGE*. AND THE MORE WE LOVE GOD WITH *ALL OUR SOUL*, THE EASIER IT WILL GET TO SHARE HIS PERSPECTIVE ON THE NEIGHBORS HE HAS *CALLED US* TO LOVE AS WELL.

This too is an area where loving God with our soul and fostering a close walk with him can help us.

The closer we get to God, the more we are inclined to see the world as he does, and that includes how he sees other people. The Lord is far from ignorant of our faults, yet he chooses to love us in spite of them. There is no amount of sin that can prevent him from seeing the part of us that remains created in his image. And the more we love God with all our soul, the easier it will get to share his perspective on the neighbors he has called us to love as well.

2. Is there someone in your life whom you struggle to see accurately? If so, what is it about them that tends to obscure who they truly are? How does the picture of them that you prefer to keep in your mind impact the way you love them? Last, what would it look like to love the real person rather than the version you have created?

This same principle applies to the second application of how loving God with your soul enables you to better love your neighbor as yourself as well.

ASSESS YOURSELF WITH GRACE

While approaching other people with an accurate view of who they are rather than how we might prefer to see them is essential for loving them well, the same is true of how we see ourselves.

As we discussed in several of the devotionals in this section, understanding how God has wired you and who he has created you to be is key to learning how we can pray, worship, and relate to him more intimately. If you have a flawed view of who you are—be it overly critical, ignorant of your faults, or anywhere in between—then your relationship with the Father will be built on a lie in the same way as it would be if you built up a false understanding of who he is. In such a circumstance, we can neither receive nor give love as the Lord desires.

And the same is true in our relationships with other people as well.

Until you get comfortable enough in your own skin to embrace who God has created you to be, then you cannot be open and honest with other people in a way that fosters a true sense of closeness with them. Even if you love your neighbor for who they truly are, if you don't know yourself, then you are asking them to love a fictionalized version of yourself in return. A relationship built on lies from either side cannot support the weight of true love and friendship.

So, if you're an introvert, own that you're an introvert and trust that God can still help you develop close, intimate, and loving relationships with other people. If you're an extrovert, embrace the ease with which you can spend time with others, but don't allow quantity to compensate for quality when it comes to the people you let get close to you.

At the same time, we must guard against becoming so comfortable with who we are that we lose sight of who the Lord is calling us to be. "This is just who I am" is a poor excuse for settling for less than the life God wants for you. And just as holding others accountable is a key component of loving our neighbors, allowing people to hold us accountable is crucial to receiving that love in return.

3. So, as we conclude for today, ask the Holy Spirit to show you any ways in which you have accepted a false understanding of who God has created you to be. Is there an area of your life where you have accepted sin as inevitable, or even justified it as an unavoidable byproduct of how you see yourself? Conversely, are you so aware of your faults that it has made it difficult to accept the gifts, talents, and sense of worth the Lord has bestowed on you? In either case, how have those misconceptions impacted your relationships with other people?

4. When you're done reflecting on those questions, look back over the previous parts of today's conversation as well and turn those thoughts into a prayer, asking God to help you love him with all your soul and, as an extension of that love, care for your neighbor as yourself.

HOW TO LOVE GOD WITH ALL YOUR MIND

In the Hebrew way of thinking, the mind was intricately bound up with the heart, which is perhaps why it does not appear in the Shema as recorded in Deuteronomy. However, in Greek thought—and, by extension, within Hellenized Judaism—the mind carried with it the notions of intelligence, disposition, and understanding. In many ways, it was essentially responsible for the way in which people understood the world around them.

As a result, loving God with your mind means looking to him and his word as that source of understanding.

In this section, we'll take a closer look at why Scripture is so important in that process before turning our attention to the ways in which giving God room to apply his word to our lives and the issues we face is a crucial part of loving him well.

To that end, we'll discuss some of the most pertinent and important issues concerning how we relate to God's word.

We'll start with a closer look at why we can trust the Bible. After all, the prevailing wisdom in our culture today—and increasingly, even among Christians—is that the Bible is more a book of moral teachings and recommendations than the infallible word of God. And until we treat his word with the respect it deserves, we can never fully love God to the extent that he deserves.

Next, we'll discuss ways that we can read the Bible better. One of the greatest obstacles to loving God with our mind is the inability to engage with his word as the living, breathing, two-edged sword that it is. Fortunately, there are some basic practices and approaches that can help Scripture come alive in ways that truly foster a closer walk with the Lord.

After that, we'll look at how we can apply Scripture to the cultural issues of our day.

At times, the relevance and applicability of God's word to those issues is clear. Other times, we need to rely on the principles it establishes to better understand how to apply it to our lives. But there will never be a topic to which the Bible is inapplicable, and embracing that truth is key to loving God with your mind.

Last, we'll discuss how to take those lessons and apply them to speaking with others on cultural issues from a biblical perspective. We'll begin with some general principles before concluding with a more specific focus on how those principles apply to loving your neighbor as yourself.

Our hope is that these devotionals will equip you with a better understanding of how to love God with your mind and a greater sense of urgency about allowing his word to renew our minds and equip us to discern his will.

As we conclude for today, though, take some time to ask God to help you think about what it means to love God with your mind.

1. When you considered the topics discussed above, what were your first reactions? Were there any that made you nervous? Did some feel like they'd come more naturally?

2. When you open the Bible, are you excited to read a message from the Lord, or does it feel more like a chore you know you're supposed to do? There will be days where the latter seems unavoidable—and that's true for us as well—but which is most common?

3. To conclude, take those thoughts and form them into a prayer, asking God to help you get excited about what he will teach you across the coming days. Write the prayer in the space below.

WHY WE SHOULD TRUST THE BIBLE

As we discussed yesterday, in the Hebrew way of thinking, the mind was intricately bound up with the heart, which set it apart from Greek thought—and by extension, within Hellenized Judaism—where the mind carried with it the notions of intelligence, disposition, and understanding. In many ways, it was essentially responsible for the way in which people understood the world around them.

As Paul described, the key to understanding the Lord's will for our lives and not being conformed to the larger views of the world is to allow God to renew our minds (Romans 12:2). Consequently, loving God with your mind means looking to him and his word as that source of understanding and renewal.

To that end, in this section we will take a closer look at why Scripture is so important in that process before turning our attention to the ways in which giving God room to apply his word to our lives and the issues we face is a crucial part of loving him well.

Unfortunately, not everyone agrees that the Bible is well suited to serve as the foundation of our worldview. In fact, an increasingly large percentage of the population would not only discount its relevance but reject its authority entirely.

After all, the prevailing wisdom of our culture is that the Bible is little more than a book of moral teachings and recommendations rather than the infallible, living word of God. And until we treat God's word with the respect it deserves, we can never fully love God as he deserves.

However, before we can discuss why we should trust the Bible and rely on its teachings to guide our worldview, it's important that you understand where you sit on this subject.

1. If someone were to ask you why you trust the Bible, what would you tell them? (If you don't trust the Bible, our hope is that this devotional will help you get there.)

While that question is a larger topic than we can cover fully in this space today,[1] many of the questions people have about the trustworthiness of Scripture pertain to two main issues.

IS TODAY'S BIBLE ACCURATE?

The first issue that often comes up when people are wrestling with how reliable and applicable the Bible is today relates to whether we can trust that the version we have is accurate to the originals. One of the key teachings of religions like Islam and Mormonism, for example, is that our Bible is a corrupted revelation, while their scriptures—the Qur'an and the Book of Mormon, respectively—are the true version of what the Lord intended to give. Are they correct?

To answer that question, we need to start by discussing where our copies of Scripture rank among other books of history.

The original books of the Bible were apparently all written on papyrus. Since this first "paper" decayed quickly, none of these original writings exist today. The same is true for the writings of Plato, Aristotle, and Julius Caesar. We simply don't have the originals of such ancient books but must rely on copies made through the centuries.

We have only nine or ten good copies of Caesar's *Gallic Wars*, none made earlier than nine hundred years after Caesar. Tacitus, the greatest ancient Roman historian, wrote fourteen books of his *Histories*; we possess only four and a half, none made earlier than the tenth century AD. We can find only five manuscripts of any work by Aristotle, none copied earlier than fourteen centuries after Aristotle wrote the originals.

---

1   For a more extensive look at why you can trust the Bible, see "Why believe the Bible?" at DenisonForum.org.

By contrast, we possess five thousand ancient Greek manuscripts of the New Testament and ten thousand copies in other ancient languages.

Fragments and parts of these copies date back as early as thirty years after the originals were written. Complete versions of the Gospels, Acts, Paul's letters, and Hebrews date to the early part of the third century. Revelation dates to the latter half of that century. Complete volumes date to the fourth century. Extensive quotations of Scripture in the letters of early Christians date to AD 100.

Those numbers are significant because we should expect some errors to creep into the handwritten copies of any ancient book. And the more copies we have, the more likely it is that we will find such errors. Watching for such common mistakes is the first step to finding them in a particular text. Then scholars are able to correct these mistakes, developing a text which is as close to the original as possible.

So how does the Bible hold up?

Miraculously well.

As a case in point, consider the Dead Sea Scrolls. Prior to their discovery in the caves at Qumran, the oldest complete copy of the Old Testament known to scholars dated to the tenth century. When a shepherd looking for a lost sheep found the first of the scrolls in 1947, the most dramatic discovery in the history of biblical archaeology and manuscripts resulted. We now possess Old Testament manuscripts dating back to the first century before Christ. The scrolls contain every book of the Old Testament except Esther. They take us a thousand years closer to the originals.

The results are amazing. There is word-for-word accuracy in more than 95 percent of the texts. The variations which remain are the results of obvious scribal errors. For instance, translators of the Revised Standard Version made only thirteen changes from the Masoretic Text for Isaiah, none affecting faith and practice.

It is clear that the scribes who transmitted the Bible across the centuries before printing was available did their work with astounding accuracy. Their work, while not perfect, was far closer than that of the manuscript copyists for any other ancient book. With the help of textual scholars, today we possess an Old Testament that is virtually identical to the originals. And the Greek New Testament we have today is likewise accurate and trustworthy.

2. Does that background impact the way you see God's word? If so, how?

When you open a Bible today, you are reading the same account that has served as the foundation of the Christian faith for thousands of years.

But that only matters if that account is still worth reading.

IS THE BIBLE STILL RELEVANT?

The second issue that tends to make people wary of trusting the Bible is doubts about its truthfulness and relevance to our culture today. After all, it matters little how closely our copies of Scripture match the originals if the content is false.

And there were plenty of false books and letters that claimed to present God's truth in those first few centuries after Christ. In response, God's people used four main criteria in evaluating which books were worthy of inclusion. (We'll focus mostly on the New Testament here, as the Old Testament was largely settled.)

First, the book must have been written by an apostle or based on his eyewitness testimony.

We can be fairly confident about the authorship of every New Testament book with the exception of Hebrews, which was and remains anonymous. However, even with Hebrews, most scholars attribute it to either a contemporary of the other New Testament authors or one of those authors himself. This criterion alone ensured that every book eventually considered Scripture was written at a time when enough people who witnessed what was written were still around to spot any lies or errors in its content.

When Matthew wrote about the Sermon on the Mount, there were people in his audience who'd heard it as well. When Luke wrote about the resurrection of Jesus and his appearances to the disciples, some of them were still around to correct him if he got it wrong.

If any of the books or letters in the New Testament had tried to distort the truth, the lies would have been quickly spotted and their credibility ruined. That they gained such wide acceptance in those early years should make it reasonable for us to accept them as well.

Second, the book must possess merit and authority in its use.

Here, it was easy to separate those writings that were inspired from those that were not. For instance, The First Gospel of the Infancy of Jesus Christ tells of a man changed into a mule by a bewitching spell but converted back to manhood when the infant Christ is put on his back for a ride (7:5–27). In the same book, the boy Jesus causes clay birds and animals to come to life (ch. 15), stretches a throne his father had made too small (ch. 16), and takes the lives of boys who tease him (19:19–24). It wasn't hard to know that such books did not come from the Holy Spirit.

Third, the book must be accepted by the larger church rather than a single congregation.

Paul's letter to the Ephesians was an early instance of a letter that became *circular* in nature, that is, read by churches across the faith. His other letters soon acquired such status. By the mid-second century, only the Gospels of Matthew, Mark, Luke, and John were accepted universally by the church, as quotations from the Christians of the era make clear. Others were not considered inspired by God.

Last, the book had to be approved by the decision of the church.

The so-called Muratorian Canon was the first list to convey the larger church's opinion regarding accepted books of the New Testament. Compiled around AD 200, it represented the usage of the Roman church at the time. The list omits James, 1 and 2 Peter, 3 John, and Hebrews, since its compiler was not sure of their authorship. All were soon included in later canons.

The list we have today was set forth by Athanasius in AD 367. His list was approved by church councils meeting at Hippo Regius in 393 and Carthage in 397. These councils did not impose anything new upon the church. Rather, they officially recognized what believers had already come to accept and use as the word of God.

By the time the councils had approved the twenty-seven books of our New Testament, these had already served as the established companion to the Hebrew Scriptures for generations. And the Bible has endured in its present state for the better part of two thousand years because every generation of believers since has recognized its relevance to their lives and authority as God's truth.

And while that relevance and authority have been increasingly challenged in recent years—at least in the West—it remains the "living and active" word of the Lord (Hebrews 4:12), and "profitable for teaching, for reproof, for correction, and for training in righteousness" (2 Timothy 3:16).

Ultimately, though, the best way to see its relevance is to try living by its truth. Make its principles the guideposts for your life and you'll experience for yourself that its words are the word of God.

To do that well, however, requires spending time reading the Bible for yourself and allowing the Holy Spirit to help you understand what is written. Sermons, Bible studies, commentaries, and articles can be great resources, but nothing can take the place of being alone with God and allowing his word to speak to you as it has to his people for thousands of years.

That will be the focus for tomorrow, though.

For now, let's conclude by going back to God in prayer and reflection.

3. We opened today by asking how you would respond if someone were to ask you why you trust the Bible. Has your answer changed? If so, how?

4. If you do believe that the Bible is God's word, does the way you live on a daily basis show evidence of that belief?

If you've grown up in the church or have been a Christian for very long, then chances are you know how you are supposed to respond to that last question. The "Sunday school answer" is of little value, however, unless it is backed up by the way you live. And we will always struggle to live in a way that honors the Lord unless we give Scripture its proper place as the foundation of how we see and interact with the larger world.

5. Finish for today by asking God to help you do just that.

HOW TO READ
THE BIBLE

Yesterday, we discussed why we can trust the Bible. We examined some of the most common challenges people bring against the authority and relevance of Scripture before concluding that, ultimately, the best way to know that God's word is true is to abide by its teachings and see the difference that it makes.

Abiding by the teachings of Scripture is much easier, however, if we know how to study it well. To that end, in this devotional we're going to look at some ways we can love God with our mind by applying the intellect and abilities he's given us to the study of his word.

With that in mind, let's begin by taking a few moments to assess how comfortable you are with delving deep into Scripture and allowing the Holy Spirit to help you apply its truth to your life.

1. When you open your Bible to read, what do you expect to happen? Do you approach Scripture with a clear goal in mind? Is your study born more from an obligatory awareness that you should spend time reading the Bible or the genuine desire to do so? When was the last time you were reading and felt like God really spoke to you through his word?

If we expect life-changing revelations every time we open the Bible to read it, chances are we're going to be disappointed. While that can happen from time to time—and the experience is incredible when it does—God is not obligated to honor our efforts to understand him better in any particular way just because we've set aside some time to read Scripture. He's still God, and sometimes the primary benefit of our study is simply getting to practice the tools at our disposal so that we are better equipped to recognize his voice when he does decide to move in a powerful way through his word.

Understanding that truth from the start is important. If we fall into the trap of chasing the high that comes from gaining new insights from the Lord, then it can be easy to start engaging with his word for the wrong reasons. Reading the Bible is simply another form of communicating with God, and just as with prayer, worship, and other forms of spending time in his presence, our goal should be drawing closer to the Lord in whatever way he decides is best.

So, with that perspective in mind, let's take a closer look at some basic principles that can enhance our understanding of Scripture and give the Spirit more tools to use in helping us draw closer to God.

THREE COMMITMENTS BEFORE READING THE BIBLE

Because the Bible is God's word rather than the product of human knowledge and study, we must be ready spiritually to hear what it says to us. To that end, it's best to begin with three personal commitments.

First, you must know the Author of this book personally.

Paul warned the Corinthians, "The natural person does not accept the things of the Spirit of God, for they are folly to him, and he is not able to understand them because they are spiritually discerned" (1 Corinthians 2:14).

If you have not committed your life to God and made Jesus your Lord, then there is still much to gain from reading the Bible. There are parts, however, that will not make sense or be as impactful as they are when the Holy Spirit is present in your life to help you understand it. And, by the same token, even if you have recognized Christ as Lord, if the Holy Spirit is not active in your life, then you should not expect to receive his help in understanding Scripture.

So, begin by making sure you have a personal relationship with God, and if you do, take the next step of surrendering every facet of your life to him. The Lord can help you do that as you read, but committing to doing so from the start can make an enormous difference.

Second, be willing to work hard.

Paul challenged Timothy, his young apprentice in the ministry, to "devote yourself to the public reading of Scripture, to exhortation, to teaching" (1 Timothy 4:13). "Devote yourself" translates a Greek term that requires previous, private preparations. Like any area of intellectual investigation, understanding and applying the Scriptures requires personal work. The more you invest, the greater the return.

It can be easy to fall into the trap of letting others study Scripture for us. After all, that's what we pay a pastor for, right? *I don't know what I'm doing, and I don't have time, so I'll just listen to my minister or Sunday school teacher and let them be the lens through which I see the Lord.*

The Bible is meant for every believer. The chance to interpret God's word for yourself is a privilege but also a responsibility. And that responsibility extends beyond simply learning more about the Lord from others.

Third, commit to obeying what you discover.

The Bible is not meant to inform our minds so much as it intends to change our lives. Jesus said, "If anyone's will is to do God's will, he will know whether the teaching is from God or whether I am speaking on my own authority" (John 7:17). Obedience leads to relationship. Faith is required.

So, decide before you open God's word that you will obey what you find there. Write your Father a blank check of obedience. He will not reveal his will as an option to consider but as an ordinance to follow. If you will not do what he says, you'll not understand what he says.

2. With which of these three steps do you tend to have the greatest difficulty? What can you do today to ensure that these commitments translate into action rather than empty words?

Once we have committed to studying God's word and obeying its teachings, we are ready to dive in and see where the Lord takes us. However, here too there are three presuppositions we need to understand if we're to study the Bible well.

THREE ASSUMPTIONS WHEN STUDYING THE BIBLE

The first assumption is that we are capable of understanding Scripture.

Luther and the Reformers were adamant that the Bible can be understood. God has given us his revelation in such a way that we can discover and apply its truths. We need not depend on creeds, councils, and church tradition, though those can be valuable resources as well. Every believer is their own priest before God and his word. That said, the degree to which that's of benefit is tied directly to the level of our reliance upon the Holy Spirit to lead and guide us, which is why not only spending time in God's word but also learning to do so well is important.

Second, use the New Testament to interpret the Old Testament.

Scripture exists to lead us to faith in Jesus (John 20:30–31). The New Testament, which reveals Christ, is therefore our means of interpreting the Old Testament, which prepares the way for him. As Jesus said repeatedly, he fulfills the Scriptures which told the world of his coming.

In other words, we will study Scripture according to the theological doctrine of progressive revelation.

We believe that God reveals himself progressively, building later revelation upon earlier truth. As a mathematics teacher must teach arithmetic before she can teach geometry, and trigonometry before she can discuss calculus, so God reveals himself progressively to us.

Upon the foundation of the Law, God spoke through his prophets. They in turn focused on the Messiah, God's personal revelation. The New Testament builds on this revelation in a person through revelation in words. The New Testament is therefore God's fullest revelation of himself to us and our means of interpreting his earlier revelation. That said, we must be wary of taking that principle to such extremes that we discount the importance and relevance of the Old Testament.

Third, make the Bible its own commentary.

Our third guiding presupposition is that the Scriptures interpret themselves. Because God's Word is unified, coherent, and fully inspired, every word is the word of God.

So the best way to study any single passage is to interpret it in light of the rest of the Bible. We will seek to compare Scripture with Scripture, interpreting the part by the whole.

3. How comfortable do you feel with the idea of being your own priest before God? Is it liberating, intimidating, or a bit of both?

Last, we'll conclude our study for today by taking a brief look at some helpful questions to ask of a text in order to enhance our understanding of God's word as we read. If you'd like to know more about this subject beyond what is discussed here, please see "Make the best preparations for Bible study" and "How can I study the Bible?" at DenisonForum.org.

ESSENTIAL QUESTIONS FOR BIBLE STUDY

The first questions we need to ask pertain to the human author of our text.

- Who wrote the passage you will study?
- What can you learn about his background, circumstances, and experiences?
- What was happening at the time he wrote the book you're about to read?

Knowing the author and his circumstances can prove invaluable in providing context to what we read.

The second question follows the first: To whom is the author writing?

- Are they believers or unbelievers?
- Persecuted or safe?
- A church, a group of churches, or an individual?
- What can you know about their circumstances, needs, and issues?

For instance, why does Mark go to such lengths to explain Jewish customs (Mark 7:2–4; 15:42) and translate Aramaic words (3:17; 5:41; etc.)? Because he is writing to Gentiles, most probably in Rome.

Why does Luke employ more medical terminology in his Gospel and in Acts than we find anywhere else in Scripture? Because he was a physician (Colossians 4:14).

Why does John begin his first letter with the claim "That which was from the beginning, which we have heard, which we have seen with our eyes, which we looked upon and have touched with our hands, concerning the word of life" (1 John 1:1)? Because every word you just read refutes incipient Gnosticism, a Greek philosophy that separated the physical from the spiritual and contended that Jesus could not be both divine and human. And this is John's purpose.

Third, what is the author's purpose?

Much of Scripture is *task theology*, produced to accomplish a specific task or purpose. If we don't understand the task at hand, we'll miss much of what the writer wants us to know and do.

Last, what is the genre?

Scripture contains a wide variety of literary styles within its pages, and understanding whether you're reading poetry or history, law or letters, apocalyptic or literal, is vital to reading a text correctly. Only then can we discover the intended meaning of the text, which is the object of all Bible study.

4. So how are you feeling about studying the Bible? Are you excited to put these principles into practice, feeling overwhelmed, or something else entirely?

However you're feeling at the moment, know that no one wants you to understand the Bible more than God does, and he stands ready and willing to speak to you if you're ready to listen. And, ultimately, that's what these tools are meant to do: help you learn to listen to God better as you read his word.

5. To close, take a few moments to pray and be honest with God about any hesitations, fears, or doubts you may have about reading the Bible. Then ask for his help, choose a passage, and jump in. As we talked about yesterday, the best way to learn how to read the Bible is by reading the Bible. Set aside some time to start today.

HOW TO APPLY SCRIPTURE TO CULTURAL ISSUES

Yesterday we examined the importance of preparing to engage with God's word and then discussed some tips for how to do so in a way that fosters both understanding and an openness to the Lord's direction. One reason it's so important to include God in every step of that process is that what he teaches us in Scripture is meant to inform the way we see every facet of our lives.

At times, the Bible's connection to the questions and issues we face will be clear. After all, teachings like *do not steal* and *do not murder* don't need a lot of help in showing their application. That said, even when one application is apparent, there is often a deeper relevance that comes to light through further study and prayer, such as when Jesus expounded upon the idea of murder in the Sermon on the Mount (Matthew 5:21–26).

At other times, we face questions that the Bible does not appear to speak to directly.

Social media, for example, obviously wasn't around in the first century. Does that mean Scripture has nothing to say on the subject? Some would argue that the same is true for issues like consensual homosexual relationships.[1]

Even when the Bible appears to be silent on an issue, though, there are clear principles we can apply to gain a better understanding of God's will and what he would have us do in response. It just takes a bit more work.

To that end, today we're going to look at two guiding principles that can help us apply the teachings of Scripture to cultural issues in a way that can enable us to better align our lives with God's will.

---

1   For more on the flaws in the argument that the Bible doesn't speak to consensual homosexuality, see "What does the Bible say about homosexuality?" at DenisonForum.org.

1. Before we begin, are there any issues where you struggle to understand what the Bible teaches? When a question arises without a clear, biblical answer, what do you do?

WHAT IS YOUR MOTIVATION?

The first step in applying biblical teaching to cultural issues is to ensure that you are approaching those issues with the right motivations.

Do you want to know what the Bible actually says about a subject, or are you looking for evidence to support your preferred understanding?

Particularly when Scripture does not speak directly to an issue, it is vital that we start that conversation with discerning God's truth as our top priority. And, while that may seem obvious, all of us are tempted on occasion to look for the answers we'd like to find rather than the answers God wants to give.

The academic term for that misplaced focus is *eisegesis*, and it essentially means to place your views on the text while ignoring context, original intent, and where a passage fits in the broader scope of Scripture. The better approach is called *exegesis*, and it refers to paying attention to those textual clues and then allowing Scripture to speak for itself.

Understanding the difference between exegesis and eisegesis is one of the most important tools for both studying Scripture and applying it to our lives in a way that honors its Author.

Some of the most heinous mistakes in Christian history have been, at least in part, the result of people practicing eisegesis over exegesis. It's crucial that we don't perpetuate that cycle.

Christian support for slavery in the antebellum South, for example, was rooted in taking the existence of slavery in the Bible, and the few passages that seem to support it, as the defining lens through which people should understand the Bible's position. Doing so completely ignores the larger themes of God's love and justice, the context of how the concept of slavery in the ancient world differed from that in the antebellum South, and the example of equality found throughout the early church.[2]

But while I would hope we all recognize the evils of slavery today and understand that the Bible does not condone that concept, understanding why people were tempted to misconstrue Scripture so that it supported their preferred ideas is crucial to not making the same mistake today.

The truth is, the Bible speaks clearly to many of our culture's most divisive issues. We just don't always like what it has to say.

And that is true for people on both sides of the political and cultural aisle.

---

[2] For more on this subject, see "What does the Bible say about racism?" at DenisonForum.org.

> 2. Are there any issues with which you find yourself wanting to agree with the culture rather than the Bible? When that tension arises, what do you do? What should you do?

Justin Giboney, a lawyer and the president of the AND Campaign, once wrote that "the Church not conforming to your ideology is a good thing not a flaw. The Church will still be around when conventional wisdom and your ideology fail you. Stand on the solid ground of Scripture."[3]

Practicing exegesis over eisegesis is the first step in doing just that. The second is to have other people in your life who are committed to doing the same.

---

[3] Justin Giboney (@JustinEGiboney), "The Church not conforming to your ideology is a good thing not a flaw," X, June 2, 2023, https://x.com/JustinEGiboney/status/1664606282161029120.

WHO IS YOUR COMMUNITY?

While taking the time to read and understand God's word on your own is a vital and irreplaceable part of understanding his truth and how to apply it to the cultural issues of our day, we are not meant to do it in isolation.

The reason we need to engage with God's word in community is not that we are somehow incapable of doing it on our own. It's just that all of us have blind spots. Unless there are other people in our lives who can point them out, then chances are good that we're going to fall short of biblical truth on some issues.

However, accepting such accountability requires a great deal of humility, more than most people possess apart from the Holy Spirit.

One reason it is so vital to surrender every part of our lives—but especially our pride—as a living sacrifice to the Lord and allow him to renew our minds is that in accepting God's view of the world, we also are better enabled to accept his view of ourselves. When we understand who we are in Christ and the unconditional love God has for us, we can better resist the temptation to tie our self-worth to our own ideas and the acceptance of others. That gets even easier, though, when we have people we can trust around us who have made the same choice.

PARTICULARLY WHEN SCRIPTURE DOES NOT SPEAK DIRECTLY TO AN ISSUE, IT IS *VITAL* THAT WE START THAT CONVERSATION WITH DISCERNING GOD'S TRUTH AS OUR *TOP PRIORITY*. AND, WHILE THAT MAY SEEM OBVIOUS, ALL OF US ARE TEMPTED ON OCCASION TO LOOK FOR THE ANSWERS WE'D *LIKE* TO FIND RATHER THAN THE ANSWERS *GOD WANTS TO GIVE*.

---

3. Do you have people in your life who are more committed to God's truth than the world's? In which parts of your life do you struggle most with making that choice?

WHO'S RIGHT?

Ultimately, applying God's word to the cultural issues of our day comes down to caring more about God being right than about us being wrong. When the latter is our focus, we are prone to looking for support rather than truth from Scripture and to surrounding ourselves with people who think as we do rather than as God does. But you can't love the Lord with all your mind if your thoughts and beliefs are more concerned with how to fit into the culture's worldview than God's.

Tomorrow we'll talk a bit more about how to approach sharing God's truth with the larger culture, but we can't give to others something we don't possess ourselves. Before we try to help those around us understand and accept a biblical perspective on an issue, we must be sure that our views align with God's word and will. Only then can we live as the kind of salt and light that Christ says we already are (Matthew 5:13–16).

4. As we conclude, go back over your answers to the first questions today. Are there any topics where you struggle to know what the Bible teaches? If so, ask God to help you discern the degree to which that struggle is the result of a lack of information or a disconnect between what we want to believe and what Scripture shows to be true.

5. When you're finished, turn those thoughts into a prayer and ask God to help you love him with your mind by prioritizing his truth, even when that means paying a price to believe it. Then ask him to bring people into your life who share that commitment and can support you in it.

DAY 23

HOW TO SHARE GOD'S TRUTHS WITH OTHERS

Yesterday we discussed that you can't love God with all your mind unless you are more committed to his truth than what you or others might prefer to believe. Having a strong foundation in Scripture is crucial to the Christian life, and it's the only place from which we can effectively try to impact our culture in a way that draws people closer to the Lord.

However, being willing to share God's truth with the world still leaves open the question of how best to do so. So our subject for today is focused less on what to believe than on how to speak up for those beliefs and share them with a culture that may not always be interested in listening.

When society or individuals make decisions that contradict God's word and will, what should we do? How do we respond? How can we make a difference? And, perhaps most importantly, to what extent is standing up for biblical truth our responsibility?

1. When you think about standing for biblical truth when that truth goes against cultural norms, what thoughts come to mind? Does it make you nervous, combative, anticipatory, or something else entirely?

2. Are there any issues or questions where you feel confident in speaking up for the Bible's perspective? Are there any where you feel ill-equipped to do so? What difference do your answers to those questions make in your approach?

While there have been countless books and articles written on how Christians should engage with our culture, Richard Niebuhr's *Christ and Culture* remains among the best, despite being published more than seventy years ago. In it, Niebuhr sketches the five ways Christians can relate their faith to their society and culture. Let's see which of these fits our calling best.

RICHARD NIEBUHR'S FIVE WAYS TO LIVE AS A CHRISTIAN

Niebuhr termed the first of his options *Christ against culture*.

This model argues that we must reject the fallen world in every way and have as little engagement with it as possible, which means largely ignoring the cultural issues of the day. However, the incarnation seems to give the lie to this approach. Jesus engaged with the issues that divided his culture and did not shy away from controversy when doing so would have kept people from knowing God's truth.

The second view is *Christ of culture*.

This model attempts to integrate the world and the word of God, the culture and the Christian faith. It blurs the distinction between the two, and whenever they come into conflict, adopts the prevailing culture as the way to understand the faith. However, the Great Commission gives the lie to this approach. Why "go therefore and make disciples of all nations" (Matthew 28:19) if the nations do not need to be evangelized and discipled?

The third is *Christ above culture*.

This approach teaches that we live in two worlds, the spiritual and the secular, and we must give each its due, as each has something of value to teach us. This view rightly emphasizes that the culture is not wholly lost and that associating with it does not invariably lead to the moral downfall of the faith. However, the problem with this approach is that it does not adequately account for the sinfulness of humanity. Nor does it do enough to transform the culture it seeks to help. While it holds Christ as supreme above the culture, it narrows the gap to a dangerous degree.

The fourth approach is *Christ and culture in paradox*.

This approach rejects the third by arguing that culture is so inherently sinful as to be beyond saving. Yet it contradicts the first (Christ against culture) by arguing that we must try. We must preach grace to law, and the gospel to the lost. We respond to the issues of our culture by presenting the gospel of salvation, for only when souls change can the world change. The problem with this approach is that it does not speak to issues the Bible itself addresses, such as the treatment of the poor or injustice in the world. In short, it does not offer a holistic worldview, whereas Scripture does.

Niebuhr's final model is *Christ transforming culture*.

Here, Christians seek to bring the biblical worldview to bear on every dimension of society for the purpose of redeeming the culture for the kingdom.

- Unlike the first model, it does not ignore the culture.
- Unlike the second, it does not adopt it.
- Unlike the third, it does not separate the two realms.
- Unlike the fourth, it seeks both the salvation of souls and the transformation of society.[1]

One challenge this model faces, however, is the difficulty of keeping salvation issues primary. While social issues are important, they must never become a higher priority than telling people about Jesus. Considering that latter part is where Christians often encounter some of the greatest opposition; resisting the temptation to skip that final step is crucial.

---

1   Richard Niebuhr, *Christ and Culture* (Harper, 1951).

3. Of the five models described above, which do you find most personally appealing? Which do you think fits best with the calling of Scripture?

Niebuhr concludes his book by arguing that, while each of the positions discussed has some redeeming qualities, there is not a single, correct answer that would fit every Christian context. Still, he admits that some are more correct than others.

So, which should we choose?

THE BIBLICAL WAY TO APPROACH CULTURE

The reason for the variance in solutions to the problem of Christ and culture is found largely in the fact that people throughout history, as well as today, are approaching it from different places.

In the early church, Christians wondered how to relate to a society that persecuted them. In the Reformation, Protestants wondered how to relate to a society that claimed to be Christian but lived as if Christ's message were irrelevant. Today, Christians are often left wondering how to relate to a society that has substituted scientific progress and a postmodern worldview for faith in God.

Each situation is likely to render different solutions not because any one answer is necessarily better than another but because each approaches the problem from a different starting place. And this lack of a common perspective does not end with how Christians are to deal with the problem of Christ and culture. It continues on to issues of faith and theology in all walks of life.

That is not to say that there are no wrong answers when it comes to matters of religious and personal importance, as there have been and will continue to be solutions that defy the truth of God. However, the search for a universally correct and applicable answer in all situations is far more likely to be true only for a given culture and a given time than for the body of Christ as a whole.

So, which approach is best for our culture?

While no solution is perfect, the *Christ transforming culture* model appears to be best suited for helping our society come to know Jesus.

Christ did not give us the option of giving up on our culture, but the culture is not going to listen if all we care about is their eternal salvation. Looking to improve the world around us is often a necessary precursor to sharing our faith, especially with younger generations. A gospel focused on escape from our world rather than transforming our world will ring hollow to many.

We'll take a closer look at how to do that tomorrow when we apply these thoughts to the context of loving your neighbor as yourself, but understanding that we cannot share God's worldview effectively without also sharing our culture's concerns for that world is the first step.

Now, that doesn't mean accepting our culture's solutions to those issues and forgetting that truth is vital to remaining a transforming force for Christ. But approaching the culture with a paternalistic and haughty attitude is going to do little to help people open up to the Lord.

That's not how Jesus approached his culture, and it's not how we should approach ours either.

4. Pick an issue that you feel comfortable defending from a biblical perspective. Now, using the *Christ transforming culture* model, how would you approach sharing God's truth in that area with those who think differently? Which factors would you emphasize, and which would you leave for later conversations?

5. While we may not always know how we will be called to stand up for biblical truth on a given day, God does. So, as we conclude, take some time and ask him to prepare and organize your thoughts so that you are ready to love God with your mind by standing up for his truth when it is challenged.

DAY 24

HOW TO LOVE YOUR NEIGHBOR WITH YOUR MIND

Over the course of our conversations on loving God with all your mind, we've focused primarily on ways to improve your personal study of the Bible and then take the insights gleaned from God's word to transform your own worldview while helping others to do the same. As with the previous sections, we'll conclude that discussion by looking at how those same principles apply to loving your neighbor as yourself.

1. Before we continue, take a few minutes to look back over your notes from the previous devotionals in this section. What, if anything, stands out to you most? When you first encountered those ideas, did you have a desire to share them with anyone else? Why do you think that was the case?

Standing up for God's truth can be intimidating when doing so places us in opposition to the larger culture around us. But if it's undertaken from the perspective of someone who is genuinely excited about what God has shown them, then it is likely to make a much more significant impact. When a biblical text or truth clearly means something to you, it is more likely that you'll be able to share it with the kind of genuine excitement and commitment that will help it mean something to others as well.

So, with that perspective in mind, let's look at how you can love your neighbor with your mind by sharing God's truth in a way that can bring about real change in the lives of those he has brought across your path.

"YOU'RE HERE TO BE SALT-SEASONING"

One of the clearest examples of what it means to embody biblical truth in your culture comes from the Sermon on the Mount, where Jesus spoke of the need to be salt and light to the lost (Matthew 5:13 MSG). The passage follows a series of beatitudes, which are essentially countercultural statements of blessing meant to instruct his followers on the kind of life they are called to live.

However, too much is made at times of the countercultural nature of Christ's words in this passage. To be sure, much of what he said, both in the Beatitudes and the instructions that followed, was countercultural. Yet, it was never Christ's purpose to be a contrarian. Rather, when it came to biblical truth, he was simply unwilling to compromise.

Jesus refused to make allowances for the greater culture in the areas that ran counter to the mission and life he was called to live. That is his call to us as well, and to further illustrate that fact, he followed the Beatitudes with a statement about the identity of those who follow him.

2. Take a few moments to read Matthew 5:13–16. What stands out most to you about the way Jesus describes his followers in this passage?

A primary purpose of salt in the ancient world was to preserve food and keep it from going bad. In a time when there was no electricity and refrigeration of any sort was often impossible, the most common way to keep meat from spoiling was to cure it with salt. As such, a key element of Jesus identifying us as *salt of the earth* is the idea that we are meant to preserve what's good and protect it from the degrading influences around us.

It's important to note, though, that we are not called *salt of the faith* or *salt of the religion.* Christ's call is not to preserve the church or Christianity—he doesn't need our help for that—but rather to preserve the world, and we can't do that in isolation from the world.

There are some today who look at the state of the culture around us and argue that Christians should withdraw from the larger society to protect our faith until a time when the world is more receptive to it. The temptation to do so is understandable. Jesus, however, was clear that we have been called to a different kind of life—one lived in the world but not of the world, as Billy Graham put it.

Loving your neighbor with your mind necessitates being willing to stand up for the faith rather than simply protect it or preserve it. And Eugene Peterson describes this calling well in his translation of this passage:

> Let me tell you why you are here. You're here to be salt-seasoning that brings out the God-flavors of this earth. If you lose your saltiness, how will people taste godliness? You've lost your usefulness and will end up in the garbage. Here's another way to put it: You're here to be light, bringing out the God-colors in the world. God is not a secret to be kept. We're going public with this, as public as a city on a hill. If I make you light-bearers, you don't think I'm going to hide you under a bucket, do you? I'm putting you on a light stand. Now that I've put you there on a hilltop, on a light stand—shine! Keep open house; be generous with your lives. By opening up to others, you'll prompt people to open up with God, this generous Father in heaven. (Matthew 5:13–16, MSG)

PREPARING FOR A PERSONAL CONVERSATION

Prompting "people to open up with God" is the primary purpose of every Christian life. Considering the degree to which so many have chosen to align with the culture over Christ, helping the lost understand not only what the Bible teaches but also why it's worth following is among the most loving pursuits we can have in this life. And even if the culture doesn't always see it that way, God does, and he says it is worth the cost.

At the end of our conversation yesterday, we encouraged you to pick a topic on which you felt comfortable defending a biblical perspective and to work through what it might look like to stand up for God's truth in that area if confronted with an opposing view.

We're going to do something similar to finish up for today, with one primary distinction.

3. Pray and ask God to bring to mind a friend or loved one who has embraced a cultural view on a subject that stands in opposition to the truth of God's word. Now, spend a few minutes thinking deeply about their perspective.

4. Ask the Lord for insights into why they believe as they do. Are they afraid to be labeled a bigot or to go against what the larger society believes? Do they genuinely think that they are correct? Are you certain they are not? If so, why?

5. Once you have prayed through those questions, ask the Lord to help you understand the best way to approach the other person to discuss the topic.

6. Finish by asking God to give you the opportunity to have that conversation and for the Spirit to guide your words as it happens. And don't minimize the importance of the Spirit's continued involvement in that process. After all, it is highly unlikely that the conversation will follow whatever path you envision. Still, giving God the tools to organize and arrange your thoughts in whatever way will prove most effective is the best place to start.

FURTHER RESOURCES

- *Respectfully, I Disagree: How to Be a Civil Person in an Uncivil Time*

HOW TO LOVE GOD WITH ALL YOUR STRENGTH

In Greek and Hebrew thought, the concept of strength referred to a person's capacity to accomplish something. So, the idea of loving God with all your strength means living for him in a way that holds nothing back. It means complete submission to the Lord, though as a choice rather than as an obligation.

In this section we'll take a closer look at how we can identify our strengths and understand our calling as we love God by surrendering both back to him.

To that end, we'll begin by looking to the beatitudes for a better understanding of what it means to be meek. That notion is often mistaken for weakness in our culture today, but the biblical concept could not be further from that idea. Rather, it speaks to the notion of strength willingly placed under the control of another. It's the picture of a warhorse consenting to be led by its rider, not because it has to but because it chooses to.

However, such meekness requires an understanding of the power being submitted.

As such, we'll also take some time to discuss the importance of spiritual gifts and the way in which loving God with our strength is largely focused on surrendering back to him the talents and abilities that he has freely given to us.

Yet, any understanding of our strengths must also be accompanied by an honest appraisal of our weaknesses. All of us have weaknesses, but when we ignore them or try to compensate for them rather than surrendering these to the Lord as well, we set ourselves up for failure.

In the final devotionals in this section, we will discuss how loving God with our strength means allowing him to use us and our story to draw others into a relationship with him. Each one of us has a story that can help others understand who God is. However, we have to give the Holy Spirit room to help us craft that story as the Lord sees fit.

But when we do, God can use our love for him to help our neighbors encounter that love in their own lives. And there can be no better use for our gifts and abilities than that.

So, as we finish for today, take some time to ask the Lord to help you prepare for these conversations.

1. When you think about your strengths and weaknesses, who are you relying on for that appraisal? Is it based on your thoughts? Those of the people around you?

2. When was the last time you asked God to help you understand your strengths and weaknesses?

3. Take some time today to do just that. Then turn those thoughts into a prayer, asking God to help you see yourself through his eyes. Write the prayer in the space below.

DAY 26

THE POWER OF MEEKNESS

In Greek and Hebrew thought, the concept of strength referred to a person's capacity to accomplish something. So, the idea of loving God with all your strength means living for him in a way that holds nothing back. It means complete submission to the Lord, though as a choice rather than an obligation.

That last part about loving God with all our strength being a choice is crucial, as it is a nearly unavoidable part of human nature to harbor at least some resentment and reticence toward the things we are forced to do. By contrast, when we have chosen to invest our time, energy, and resources in a task, it becomes easier to pursue it with abandon. That is the kind of devotion God is looking for from his followers, and it is the kind of devotion he has shown toward us as well. After all, nothing speaks to the all-encompassing commitment of the Lord more than Christ's willingness to die to pay for our sins and provide a path to restored communion with the Lord.

If that was the measure of God's devotion to us, how can we give him any less in return?

To that end, in this section we'll take a closer look at how we can identify our strengths and understand our calling as we love God by surrendering both back to him.

And we'll start by looking at what it means to be meek.

1. When you hear the term *meekness*, what comes to mind? Is it a quality that you associate more with strength or with weakness?

The biblical understanding of what it means to be meek is quite different from the predominant view in our culture today. As such, we've largely lost sight of one of the most significant qualities God is looking for in his followers.

Our purpose today is to rediscover that idea and see how it forms the foundation of what it means to love God with all your strength.

FOUR CHARACTERISTICS OF BIBLICAL MEEKNESS

In the Sermon on the Mount, Jesus told his disciples, "Blessed are the meek, for they shall inherit the earth" (Matthew 5:5). The Greek word translated here as "meek" is *praus*, and it has historically been understood as something akin to humility.

Unfortunately, humility is a concept that our culture understands about as well as it does meekness. We live in a society that often assigns value based on performance and production. Our natural bent is often toward trying to impress those around us. However, it's hard to want to impress people at the same time as being humble. So, to help us bridge that gap, let's look at four different aspects of what it means to be biblically meek.

First, meekness is not a false humility born of self-deprecation, in which we overvalue our faults to the neglect of what we do well.

This false humility often manifests in an inability to take a compliment, hesitance to embrace the areas in which we're gifted, and looking down on others when they don't share this attitude of self-deprecation. As we'll discuss toward the end of today's devotional, all of us have been created in the image of God and blessed with incredible gifts to use in advancing his kingdom. It would be strange, then, for Jesus to say that the key to inheriting that kingdom is ignoring or minimizing those attributes.

At the same time, though, Scripture is clear that taking self-serving pride in those gifts is dangerous as well. That's what makes the second quality of biblical meekness so important.

Second, meekness enables us to see ourselves as God sees us.

All of us are tempted to judge ourselves based on the judgments of others from time to time. For many in our culture, this approach becomes the primary lens through which they see themselves, and that tendency is at the root of many of the problems we face as a society. The circular torment of obsessing over what others think leads us to cater our lives to their judgment.

And even if you reject that basic premise and try not to care what others think, then you are still largely basing your identity on the views of other people. You're just taking those opinions and doing the opposite.

Conversely, when we allow God to be the one who establishes our identity, we can know true peace and contentment while being better positioned to embrace a humble, meek approach to our lives.

So how does God see us?

While a complete list would be too long to include here, some important aspects are:

- Sinners who fall short of God's glory (Romans 3:23)
- People worthy of eternity in hell (Romans 6:23)
- Individuals whom God loved so much that he deemed their salvation worth the cost of his Son (John 3:16)
- If you're a Christian, then you are the adopted child of God and co-heir with Christ (Romans 8:16–17)

Seeing ourselves as God sees us allows us to acknowledge our faults and our gifts without defining ourselves by either. That, in turn, frees us to be truly humble.

Biblical meekness, however, is not just about how we see ourselves.

Third, see others as God sees them.

Just as we learned in the previous step to see ourselves as God sees us, defining our identity by our relationship with him, we must extend that same grace to others as well. As Paul instructed the Ephesians, "Be kind to one another, tenderhearted, forgiving one another, as God in Christ forgave you" (Ephesians 4:32).

This kind of forgiveness requires a level of humility that does not come naturally to our fallen nature. It's also not possible if our humility is based on anything other than our standing before the Lord.

Only true humility—biblical meekness—will enable us to model to others the kind of forgiveness God has shown toward us.

Fourth, see your gifts as God sees them.

The final step in positioning ourselves to experience the blessing Jesus promised to the meek is to see our gifts and abilities as God sees them.

David Saylor has, perhaps, my favorite definition of praus: "power put under control."

SEEING OURSELVES AS GOD SEES US ALLOWS US
TO *ACKNOWLEDGE* OUR FAULTS AND OUR GIFTS
WITHOUT DEFINING OURSELVES BY EITHER. THAT,
IN TURN, FREES US TO BE TRULY *HUMBLE*.

He likens it to a powerful stallion submitted to the control of its rider.[1]

The stallion's strength, speed, and abilities are not lessened because it has learned to follow its rider's lead. Rather, in many ways they are enhanced because its wild nature is more easily focused toward a particular end.

The same happens when we take the gifts and abilities God has instilled in each of us and present them back to him as a living sacrifice (Romans 12:1).

True meekness means embracing our gifts and talents as a blessing from God, then submitting them to his service.

When we do this, genuine humility is no longer an ideal we have to pursue but instead a natural byproduct of our walk with God.

CHOOSE TO SUBMIT YOUR STRENGTHS TO GOD

Today we've examined four different aspects of what it means to be biblically meek. As we've seen, each comprises a different, yet equally vital, aspect of genuine humility.

Choosing to submit our God-given strengths back to our creator rather than trying to ignore or diminish them, then learning to define both ourselves and others through his eyes alone, are crucial steps to loving God with all our strength. However, they are also often easier said than done.

---

1   David Saylor, "The Sermon Jesus Preached," sermon, First Baptist Church Manchester, CT, March 26, 2017, https://sermons.logos.com/sermons/170118-march-26-2017-morning-worship.

2. So, as we close for today, take some time to pray and ask the Holy Spirit to show you which of the four steps seems most difficult for you to practice on a daily basis, and why.

3. When you're done, ask the Lord to show you some practical steps you can take to help overcome those difficulties.

4. Last, ask God to help you live in such a way that you can experience the blessing and freedom of biblical meekness.

UNDERSTANDING YOUR STRENGTHS

Yesterday we discussed how embracing a biblical concept of meekness—recognizing our gifts and then submitting them back to God to use as he desires—is vital to loving God with all our strength. However, we can't submit what we don't understand that we possess.

To that end, today we're going to look at the concept of spiritual gifts and take a test to see where God has gifted you, if you haven't done one recently. The assessment is not intended to replace the Spirit's direction in your life, but if you pray through the questions and answer them based on what is true rather than what you wish were true, you will come away with a better understanding of what areas your gifting resides in.

1. Before reading further, take our free spiritual gift assessment.[1] Once that's completed, write down your top three to four spiritual gifts.

---

1   https://www.whataremyspiritualgifts.org/

Knowing your gifting, however, is of little importance unless it is paired with the knowledge of how to use your spiritual gifts well. So we'll spend the remainder of our time today exploring how we can discern the best ways to use our spiritual gifts for God's glory.

WHAT DOES THE BIBLE SAY ABOUT SPIRITUAL GIFTS?

READ 1 CORINTHIANS 12:12–31

The passage of Scripture most often used when discussing spiritual gifts is 1 Corinthians 12:12–31. Here, we find Paul's statement that every Christian has been gifted in a unique way. Moreover, he demonstrates how vital it is that we use our gifts according to God's calling since, otherwise, the body of Christ cannot function as the Lord intends.

In many ways, this teaching is the continuation of a theme that runs throughout much of the letter. That context informs our understanding of both how Paul talks about spiritual gifts and how we should see our individual gifts within the larger body of believers.

For example, in the preceding chapter of 1 Corinthians, Paul describes division in the church because the wealthy Christians were consuming all the food and wine at the Lord's Supper before the poor believers could get there. It's essentially a depiction of one group selfishly using something that was meant to honor God and bring them all together.

By pivoting from that passage to a discussion about spiritual gifts, Paul drives home that our gifts, like every other part of our lives, are meant to be used for God's glory rather than our own. The Lord has given us the freedom to choose the extent to which we'll live in accordance with those priorities, but he is also clear that there are consequences for making the wrong choice.

If we forget why we've been gifted in the first place, then it's easy to begin viewing those gifts through a more selfish lens. No gift is any more vital or God-inspired than the rest, but that's how it can appear if we take a worldly view of our spiritual blessings. That's why Paul writes about gifts in the context of the larger community of faith.

That corporate perspective on our personal gifts is an important message, and one rightfully used to encourage believers. However, that's not the end of the conversation for Paul.

READ 1 CORINTHIANS 12:4–11

The verses discussed above are preceded by several more in which Paul describes the nature of spiritual gifts from a more general perspective.

In 1 Corinthians 12:4–11, he notes that every gift—and the ones named in these verses do not form an exhaustive list—comes from the Holy Spirit, and that these gifts must be empowered by the Spirit in order to function correctly.

The Greek word used in verse 11 to describe that empowerment is *energeo* and it literally means "to energize" or "to be at work." The basic idea is that our spiritual gifts can't work as God intends unless they are consistently powered by the Holy Spirit's presence in our lives.

That emphasis on how the gifts work best is important because our gifts don't magically appear at the moment of our salvation. Nor do they go away entirely if we're not walking with the Lord. Rather, God gave you your gifts when he knit you together in your mother's womb. They've always been part of your life and, typically, correspond pretty closely to your personality.

While ranking low on a particular gift does not mean the Lord cannot use you in that capacity, all of us have some gifts that come more naturally than others. For example, regardless of your score on evangelism, you are still called to share your faith, but it could be that, to know how to do so, you would benefit from the example of those with this gift.

You see, God had a plan for the role he wants you to play in his kingdom from the very beginning, and he gifted you to fill that role well. Those gifts, however, weren't fully actualized until the Holy Spirit came into your life. And they will not remain optimized apart from the Spirit's power.

READ GALATIANS 5:1–15

Paul gives us more insight into why that's the case in Galatians 5.

In this chapter, Paul uses circumcision to talk about the larger issue of self-justification. The notion that people had to earn their salvation—or justify God's free gift of it after being saved—was a big problem in the early church. The Jews built much of their society around the idea of following the law well enough to attain the Lord's favor, and that idea carried over into the first generations of Christians as well.

Paul had to deal with this heresy in most of the places where he ministered, and he wrote about it frequently because people who held that belief would often corrupt the churches he started after he had moved on to plant others.

By the time he wrote Galatians, you can tell he was fed up with it. And a big part of his frustration was that the principle of self-justification tended to corrupt every facet of a believer's walk with God, including their spiritual gifts.

In verse 4 he describes why that's the case: Those who continue to try to justify themselves before God "are severed from Christ . . . you have fallen away from grace." That phrase is a bit misleading in English, though.

The Greek word used here for "severed" (*katargeo*) more literally translates as "to make idle." The idea is not that believers are in danger of losing their salvation; rather, they've rendered the life-giving grace of God inactive. They've essentially hit the off switch on their connection to the Holy Spirit. And, as Paul made clear in 1 Corinthians, our spiritual gifts can't function the way God intends unless the Spirit is the one making them work.

READ GALATIANS 5:16–21

However, trying to justify our own standing before the Lord and power our own spiritual gifts is not the only way we can sever our connection to the Holy Spirit. Later on in Galatians 5, Paul describes another mistake believers can make to reach the same place spiritually.

In verses 16–21, Paul describes people who think they have a relationship with God but whose lives don't reflect his presence. He frames the discussion as a battle between the Spirit and the flesh, noting that one cannot serve both. His focus, however, is less on individual sins—though he is clear that no sin should be taken lightly—and more on the habitual kind.

In this passage, Paul is referencing those whose lifestyles are still defined by the sins of their former lives. Such sins inhibit the Holy Spirit's influence on a person, and, as with those who try to justify themselves, the implication is that one's gifts will lack the Spirit's power.

Paul goes so far as to warn that those who lack the Spirit's power as described in these passages should examine whether they are actually saved (Galatians 5:19–21). While Scripture is clear that it's not our responsibility to judge the status of another person's salvation—only the individual and God can truly know that—Jesus did give us some basic guidelines when he talked about how a tree is recognized by its fruit (Matthew 7:15–19), an idea that Paul picks up in the following verses.

Paul gives us a bit more insight into what that fruit looks like toward the end of Galatians 5.

In verses 22–23, he writes that "the fruit of the Spirit is love, joy, peace, patience, kindness, goodness, faithfulness, gentleness, self-control." This fruit is a vital part of living out the spiritual gifts God has given us, but each characteristic will only be present in our lives when we are walking with the Spirit.

After all, some of the spiritual gifts can be pretty rotten without the fruit of the Spirit.

- Discernment without gentleness and kindness devolves into judgment.
- Evangelism without love becomes condemnation.
- Giving without faithfulness is done for our glory instead of God's.
- Serving without joy and peace does little to advance the gospel or minister to other people.
- Leadership without gentleness and self-control turns people into tyrants.

And the same basic principle applies to every one of the spiritual gifts.

Conversely, if we are connected to the Spirit, then our gifts will function as they should because they will be supported by the fruit of his presence in our lives.

- Shepherding with patience leads to discipleship.
- Hospitality with joy and kindness makes others feel welcome.
- Exhortation with love and goodness helps people accept your message.
- Mercy with peace and gentleness helps the hurting find comfort.

God designed our gifts to work in conjunction with the character and qualities his Spirit develops in those who walk with him. But if we let him, Satan will use for evil what God intends for good. While the Lord can still redeem our mistakes and bring a measure of blessing out of them, the kingdom would be much better off if he didn't have to.

WHEN YOU DISCOVER YOUR GIFTING

Our gifts are tools from God, intended to help us and others grow in our walk with him, but far too often they go underappreciated and underrecognized. Part of the reason is that it can be easy to assume that you are gifted in whatever way you are currently serving.

The reality is, however, that the needs of our church or of those around us do not necessarily constitute our calling. And while that doesn't mean we should only serve in the areas where we are gifted, understanding the ways in which you can best align your God-given abilities with the needs of the kingdom can help you find a sense of joy and purpose in serving him that can otherwise be missing in our lives.

2. Understanding our spiritual gifts and then submitting them to the Lord's direction are integral parts of what it means to love God with all our strength. So, as we conclude for today, take some time to ask the Spirit to help you understand not only what your gifts are but why he chose to give them to you.

3. Then pray that the Lord would grant you the sense of peace and contentment we discussed on day 11 in regard to your gifting.

4. Last, ask God to make you attuned to any opportunities he brings your way to use your gifts for his glory. And know that this should not be a one-time conversation. Rather, it should continue throughout the day and throughout your week as God uses your experiences to help you better understand and submit your strengths to him.

FURTHER RESOURCES

- *What Are My Spiritual Gifts? How to Discover, Understand, and Apply Your Spiritual Gifts*

DAY 28

UNDERSTANDING YOUR WEAKNESSES

Yesterday we discussed the nature of our spiritual gifts and how submitting them back to God is a key step in loving him with all our strength. Yet, any understanding of our strengths must be accompanied by an honest appraisal of our weaknesses. All of us have them, but when we ignore them or try to compensate rather than surrendering those to the Lord as well, we set ourselves up for failure.

The nature of those weaknesses, however, can be as unique as our gifts. There are some basic guidelines in Scripture for how to address them: flee from temptation (1 Corinthians 6:18), humble yourself before God (Proverbs 16:18), avoid spending time with people set on sinning (Proverbs 4:14–15), and so on. But what works for me may not translate directly to your life. After all, Satan desperately wants us to fail, and he's too cunning to take a one-size-fits-all approach to temptation (1 Peter 5:8).

So how do we surrender our weaknesses to God and learn to rely on him to help us remain committed to him in the face of sin?

It starts with being aware of the ways in which you are most likely to be tempted.

1. Take a few moments to pray and ask God to show you any areas of your life where you are particularly vulnerable to sin. Are there any sins that, no matter how many times you stumble and repent, always seem to come back around? Is there a temptation that you've learned to give a wider berth than others seem to need?

With those thoughts in mind, let's turn our attention to how Jesus approached this issue with someone who was particularly unaware of their vulnerability until it was too late.

WHEN YOUR WEAKNESS KEEPS YOU AWAY FROM GOD

The story of the rich young ruler appears in three of the four Gospels, each with some additional details about the man who approached Jesus full of confidence but who left in abject sorrow.

Luke 18:18 tells us that he was a *ruler*, someone in charge of a Jewish synagogue. He was a layman elected by his peers to this position. He governed the affairs of their local synagogue, selected the preachers and readers for the services, presided over the elders (a kind of board of directors), and generally ran the institution. This position was a tremendous honor and a great religious accomplishment.

Matthew 19:20 says that he was young. He had to be at least thirty to be a synagogue ruler and was probably just that, making him around the same age as Jesus. Such success early on must have left him with great expectations for where the rest of his life would lead.

And he was wealthy. In fact, Matthew 19:22 says that he had great possessions. The word means that he possessed fields, houses, and other property as well as great financial means. A real estate tycoon, we would say today.

But all his success was not enough for his soul: "Teacher, what good deed must I do to have eternal life?" (v. 16).

Like most in his day, he thought that eternal life is something we get from the things we do. So, Jesus showed him that this wouldn't work. "Keep the commandments," he told him (v. 17). He listed the sixth, seventh, eighth, ninth, and fifth, then he summarized them with Leviticus 19:18, "Love your neighbor as yourself" (vv. 18–19).

The man said that he'd kept all these. So Jesus showed him that he had not: "If you would be perfect, go, sell what you possess and give to the poor, and you will have treasure in heaven; and come, follow me" (v. 21).

But the man wouldn't do it: "When the young man heard this he went away sorrowful, for he had great possessions" (v. 22). He was the only man in all the Scriptures who came to Jesus in faith and left sad.

2. Look back again at the questions we asked to start today. Are those sins and temptations keeping you from complete commitment to Christ? If so, how can you follow Christ's command to the rich young ruler?

WHAT POSSESSES YOU?

For this man, the thing keeping him from a life fully devoted to Christ was his money. Note, though, that this was the only person Jesus ever asked to sell all his possessions and give them to the poor. Not Nicodemus, or Zacchaeus, or Joseph of Arimathea, three famously wealthy men of the Gospels. Just this man.

The reason was simple: His possessions possessed him. He had to sell them to gain his soul. This is not a condition for everyone to follow Jesus. But it was essential for this man.

Perhaps the issue keeping you from complete commitment to Jesus isn't your possessions, though. If not, what is it? What possesses you?

Is it your career?

Your vocational ambitions, which you are afraid will be compromised if you fully follow Jesus? Do you fear that you won't get the promotion, or the position, or the status you want so much? If so, ask yourself: Is it really wise to trade a forty-year career for the eternal rewards reserved only for those who fully follow Jesus? Is this a good career move?

Is it your time?

I don't need to sell my possessions, but I do need to sell my calendar. I must occasionally remember that the one who died for my sins loves me and knows far better than I do how to make my life significant. Every day I must surrender that day's plans and agendas to his lordship. What about you?

Is it your friends?

When you have to choose between popularity with them and pleasing Jesus, does Jesus lose? Remember that Jesus died for you—did they? Would they? Remember that he knows the future, and all that is best for you—do they? Remember that he will be there for you through the hardest times of your life—will they? Remember that your eternal reward in heaven is based on pleasing Jesus, not popularity with your friends. Is putting friends before Jesus the right thing to do?

Is it your family?

Under God, my family is my first priority. I will put them before my work, my ambitions, and my friends. But will I put them before God? Will you? Can God ask you to make a sacrifice that will cause them to sacrifice as well? Know that he loves your family even more than you do. But know also that following him means putting him before everyone else, even them.

Have you done this?

DON'T MINIMIZE YOUR WEAKNESSES; SURRENDER THEM

Ultimately, all of us have areas where Christ's call to turn them over to him is especially difficult. Mine may be different from yours, just as yours may be different from those of other people in your life.

One temptation common to all of us, though, is deceiving ourselves into thinking that our areas of vulnerability really aren't that big of a deal.

After all, we can always find someone else who appears to struggle more, sin more, and give less of their lives to God than we do. And you may be completely accurate in that assessment. But God doesn't care.

Scripture is clear that each one of us is judged against the perfection of God rather than the sins of other people (Matthew 5:48). And we will all fall short of that standard.

WE WILL NEVER LOVE GOD WITH ALL OUR *STRENGTH*
UNTIL WE LOVE HIM ENOUGH TO *SEEK* HIS STRENGTH
IN OUR AREAS OF *WEAKNESS*.

---

3. So, as we conclude for today, think once again on the sins and temptations God brought to your mind earlier. Ask for his help in giving them over to him. Rigorously apply the guidelines we mentioned at the start of today's devotional to this area of your life and ask the Holy Spirit to convict you whenever you are tempted to compromise them.

We will never love God with all our strength until we love him enough to seek his strength in our areas of weakness.

But, when we do, something amazing happens: He's able to take our weaknesses and turn them into strengths by using them to keep us closer to him and to amplify our witness to others who struggle in that same area (2 Corinthians 12:9).

The latter part of that redemption will be part of our focus for tomorrow, but for now, let's finish by going to God once again in prayer.

4. Take what the Lord has shown you about your areas of weakness and vulnerability to sin and turn those thoughts into a prayer. Be sure to write it down as it is likely a prayer you will need to pray in the future as well.

THE POWER OF PERSONAL TESTIMONY

Yesterday we discussed that a key part of loving God with all your strength is the willingness to surrender your weaknesses to him. When we do, he can take those weaknesses and turn them into strengths by using them to enhance our witness.

Examining what that looks like will be our focus for today.

While God can use your gifts to do amazing things for his kingdom, it's your life and personal testimony that can be the greatest strength we have to offer him.

1. When it comes to sharing your testimony, how comfortable are you with telling others about what God has done in your life? Do you think that's something you could do in about five to ten minutes? Have you given much thought to which parts of your story you might emphasize?

We'll talk more about some practical tips for shaping your story toward the end of today's devotional, but let's begin by looking at why our willingness to do so is so important.

ALWAYS BE PREPARED

When famed evangelist William Carey was first seeking support from a group of

Baptist leaders to go to India, he was told to sit down because "when God pleases to convert the heathen, he'll do it without consulting you or me."[1]

While I hope that you can see the error in such evident disregard for the Great Commission (Matthew 28:18–20), it can still be easy to live as though there were some truth to that misguided minister's words.

After all, it's rare for us to be God's only option when it comes to sharing the gospel with those who desperately need to hear it. There are more than two billion Christians in the world, so the chances that you're the only one someone will meet are pretty low, especially if you live in the West.

However, just because you aren't the only person God can use doesn't mean you aren't the one he wants to use. That fact can be difficult to accept, though, if it feels like we're not his best option.

If you don't have the gift of evangelism or much experience in sharing your testimony— or even if you do—the thought of sharing the gospel with other people can feel quite daunting. But as we discussed when we looked at spiritual gifts, you don't have to be gifted in evangelism to be called to tell people about Christ.

It could be that there is something in your story the Holy Spirit knows will resonate with the other person and help to tear down whatever barriers they've built up against the good news of Jesus. In that situation, you very well might be God's best option for breaking through and helping to lead someone to salvation. The question then becomes whether you will be ready when the Lord brings that opportunity your way.

---

1   "Wiliam Carey: Father of Modern Protestant Missions," *Christianity Today*, August 8, 2008, https://www.christianitytoday.com/2008/08/william-carey/.

2. Can you think of a time when you were given the chance to share the gospel with someone? How did you feel at that moment? Looking back on it, is there anything you'd do differently?

So, what steps can we take today to help equip us for those opportunities in the future?

THREE WAYS TO BE READY TO SHARE YOUR STORY

The first step is to make sure that you're walking closely enough with God to recognize when the Holy Spirit prompts you to do something.

As we talked about in the section on loving God with your soul, the best way to recognize God's voice is to listen to him often. So, make it a daily habit to spend time praying and setting aside the necessary space to study Scripture. When we do, we will be better prepared to listen and understand when the Lord leads us to share our faith.

And, considering that we need the Spirit's help most while we're in the midst of those conversations, becoming familiar with his presence in the less stressful moments is of great importance.

Second, place as many tools as possible at the Holy Spirit's disposal.

When Jesus promised his disciples that they didn't need to worry when put on trial because the Holy Spirit would speak for them, he did not mean that we would essentially become God's puppets in those moments (Mark 13:11). You're still you when called to speak on behalf of the Lord.

More often than not, the way that played out in Scripture was the Spirit taking the knowledge a person already possessed and weaving it together in a way that best fit the needs of the moment.

For example, when the disciples were called before the Sanhedrin in Acts, their defense was almost always based on the biblical history they would have grown up studying. There was no new information in what they said. What was novel about it was how the Spirit was able to retell that story in a way that pointed clearly to Jesus.

And it's the same with us today.

While God is absolutely capable of giving us new revelations and previously unknown knowledge, that doesn't seem to be how he operates. As such, every bit of biblical insight and theological truth we learn adds more resources for the Spirit to use.

And when the time comes to share it, we can trust God to give us thoughts and answers that may sound as new to us as they do to the person with whom we are speaking. That will only happen, though, if we ask the Spirit to take the lead and then trust him to do so.

That approach doesn't guarantee we'll say everything correctly or that the other person will respond with faith—they are not God's puppets either—but it does mean that we will have done everything we can to allow the Lord to move and work through us. To put it in our present context, it will mean that we have effectively loved him with all our strength.

Once we have, the final step is to leave it in God's hands and ask him to help us prepare for any follow-up conversations or new opportunities to share the gospel.

This time of reflection is important because the Lord has a way of helping us grow stronger in our faith while teaching us new truths when we share his good news with others. And as he does, it just adds more resources for him to use in the future; resources that can help us grow in our walk with him and equip us to help others do the same.

Moreover, thinking back on your experiences can help you hone your approach and learn from anything you may wish you had done differently. While some conversations may stretch longer, being able to tell your story in about five minutes can make a huge difference in the effectiveness of your testimony. Since it's likely that five minutes will require leaving some stuff out, learning to allow the Holy Spirit to guide that process and let you know what was most impactful can improve your ability to share your story again in the future.

At the same time, what is relevant and applicable to one person might not be to another. That's why it's so important to let the God who knows the other person's heart and mind be the one who decides which parts of your story to emphasize. Giving God the freedom to work through you rather than approaching each situation with a rote script in your head will yield a much more effective presentation of the gospel, and that gets easier to do the more you do it.

So, allow the Holy Spirit to help you learn from both your mistakes and your successes to grow in your ability to understand how the Lord has worked in your life and how to relate that message to those with whom he calls you to share it.

3. With that in mind, take some time to pray and ask God to help you hone your testimony into a story he can use to help others know him better. Write down any key moments or thoughts he brings to mind.

4. Then, when you're done, commit to asking a friend or family member if you can share your testimony with them. Be sure to include God in that conversation as well, as it could be he plans to use it as more than just an opportunity to practice. After all, it's surprising how often even the people closest to us don't fully grasp all that the Lord has done in our lives. Let's correct that today.

HOW TO LOVE YOUR NEIGHBOR WITH ALL YOUR STRENGTH

In this section, we've discussed what it means to love God with all your strength. We've seen how that endeavor has to start with embracing a posture of biblical meekness in which we both understand our strengths and acknowledge the gifts God has given us, while at the same time submitting those gifts back to him as a knight submits to a king or a war horse submits to its rider.

We've also taken the time to gain a greater understanding of both our spiritual gifts and the areas in which we are weak, before discussing how the Lord can use both to help shape our testimony in a way that can help others know him better.

Now, as we come to the conclusion of not only this section but the study as a whole, we're going to spend some time further contemplating what it means to love your neighbor as yourself in the context of loving God with every facet of our lives, but particularly when it comes to loving him with our strength.

1. Before we begin, take a few moments to look back over your responses to the previous questions in this section. Remind yourself of the ways God has gifted you and of the areas in which you are most in need of his help. Think back on how those factors have influenced the story of his impact on your life that he's equipped you to share with others.

With that context in mind, we're ready to look at one of Scripture's clearest examples of what it means to love your neighbor as yourself while, perhaps, seeing this familiar story in a new light.

WHO IS YOUR NEIGHBOR?

2. Take a few minutes to read Luke 10:25–37. Ask God to help you see the parable of the good Samaritan with fresh eyes. Then write down whatever aspects of the story stand out to you most.

One point we've emphasized throughout these devotionals is that our love for God is not complete until that love flows to our neighbors as well. As we see in Luke 10, though, the concept of who we should consider to be our neighbor has proved to be open to interpretation throughout much of history.

In the first century, the identity of one's neighbor had been limited within Judaism to only include one's fellow Israelites or other resident aliens.[1] That said, the fact that the lawyer asked Jesus to define the identity of his neighbor perhaps indicates that the issue was not as resolved by this time as it once was. Either way, though, the answer Jesus gave was surely beyond the pale of Jewish orthodoxy in the first century.

Jews and Samaritans were both descended from the people of Israel. However, after the Jews were exiled by Assyria, a remnant remained in the promised land, and mixed marriages produced by their union with the area's other inhabitants led to the creation of the Samaritan people. When the Jews finally returned from exile, the Samaritans offered to help them rebuild Jerusalem but were rebuffed on account of those marriages. Then, to firmly cement the mutual hatred between the two groups, the Jews conquered the Samaritans during the Maccabean period and forced them into service until the Romans then conquered the Jews and ended that arrangement.

---

1   Jacob Milgrom, *Leviticus 17–22*, The Anchor Yale Bible Commentaries, (Yale University Press, 2000).

As a result, despite their common ancestry and many similar theological views—including the hope for a Messiah—the relationship between the two people groups devolved to the point that their mutual hatred and distrust were an accepted part of life during this time.

Jesus could not have chosen a more unlikely hero for his story, or one better suited to making his point.

You see, when Christ told of a Samaritan stopping near the man on the brink of death, the only good his original audience might have expected to come from him was putting the man out of his misery. The idea that he would not only take the man to get help but then take additional steps to ensure that he made a full recovery was beyond belief.

So, when Jesus asked who the neighbor was in this story, even the self-righteous scribe was forced to admit that it was the Samaritan—though he was unable to use that title, referring to him only as "the one who showed him mercy" (Luke 10:37).

3. When you think about this story, what lessons do you think Christ wanted us to learn from the Samaritan's actions regarding what it means to love our neighbor? How might those translate to our culture today?

While there is evidence in this story of the Samaritan loving the injured man with his heart, mind, and soul, what stands out most in the story is how he loved him with his strength. In addition to teaching us how to identify our neighbor—in this context, essentially anyone whom God prompts us to help—this parable also has a great deal to say about what it means to love others as an outpouring of the love for God that we have discussed in this section.

MODELING GOD'S LOVE

The first lesson we can learn from this story is that when Jesus speaks about loving your neighbor, he envisions a love that gives without the expectation of reimbursement or personal reward.

As Kierkegaard notes, whether a deed demonstrates love depends largely on how it is done.[2] Consequently, Jesus illustrates that the true neighbor is one who acts with compassion toward others without the expectation of personal benefit.

That is not to say it would be wrong for the neighbor to be reimbursed, but if our primary motivations for loving others are selfish in nature, then we are not truly being a neighbor to anyone. If God has given us the resources to help and has called us to use them to that end, then our love for the Lord necessitates that we do so.

Second, truly loving another as we love ourselves can, at times, necessitate a degree of commitment that asks more of us than we are naturally inclined to give.

In addition to going out of his way to help the man get on the path to recovery, the Samaritan demonstrated a dedication to continuing to care for the man to whatever extent was necessary. As such, it seems clear that Christ's definition of neighborly action includes more than a partial commitment.

However, considering that we are called to be fully committed to loving God, it should not come as a surprise that he calls us to be fully committed to loving our neighbor as well.

A key part of submitting our strengths to the Lord is that he not only gets to tell us when to use them but also when it's time to stop. Making such an open-ended commitment requires a great deal of faith on our part that God will not ask more of us than we are capable of giving. He gets to be the one to draw that line, though, and we are not going to give him that freedom unless our love and devotion to the Lord is absolute.

4. So, as we finish this lesson and this series, take some time to ask God to show

---

2   Søren Kirkegaard, *Works of Love* (Oxford University Press, 1946; Harper Perennial Modern Classics, 2009).

you any ways in which your love for him falls short of that standard. Is there a particular aspect of loving God that we have discussed—heart, soul, mind, or strength—that is particularly difficult to surrender to the Lord? Is there one that comes more naturally than the rest?

5. When you are finished, turn those answers into a prayer, asking God to help you love him with all your heart, soul, mind, and strength, and then extend that love to any neighbor he brings along your path.

ABOUT DENISON MINISTRIES

DENISON MINISTRIES is a nonprofit that equips and disciples followers of Jesus Christ with biblical truth, empowering them to think critically, live faithfully, and serve intentionally to cultivate flourishing communities. The ministry accomplishes that through four distinct brands:

- **Denison Forum (denisonforum.org)** offers a biblical and redemptive perspective on current events through The Daily Article email newsletter and podcast, *The Denison Forum* Podcast, and many books and online resources.

- **Christian Parenting (christianparenting.org)** provides practical and spiritual resources, including an expansive podcast network, to help parents raise children to know and love the Lord.

- **First15 (first15.org)** leads Christians into a transformative personal encounter with God through devotional readings, worship videos, and guided prayers.

- **Foundations (foundationswithjanet.org)** offers Bible studies for individual and small-group use.

Learn more at DenisonMinistries.org.

ABOUT DENISON FORUM

In 2009, Jim Denison, PhD, and Jeff Byrd founded Denison Forum in Dallas, Texas. Their goal was to encourage spiritual awakening while equipping believers to engage with the issues and news of the day. Jim Denison's The Daily Article is distributed via email, social media, and podcast to hundreds of thousands of culture-changing Christians daily.

To learn more visit DenisonForum.org.

ABOUT DR. RYAN DENISON

RYAN DENISON, PHD, is the Senior Editor for Theology at Denison Forum, where he contributes writing and research to many of the ministry's productions. He holds a PhD in church history from BH Carroll Theological Institute after having earned his MDiv at Truett Seminary. Ryan has also taught at BH Carroll and Dallas Baptist University.

He and his wife, Candice, live in East Texas and have two children.

ABOUT DR. JIM DENISON

JIM DENISON, PHD, is a cultural theologian and the founder and CEO of Denison Ministries. He speaks biblically into significant cultural issues through *The Daily Article* at DenisonForum.org. He is the author of over 30 books, including *The Coming Tsunami: Why Christians Are Labeled Intolerant, Irrelevant, Oppressive, and Dangerous—and How We Can Turn the Tide; Respectfully, I Disagree: How to Be a Civil Person in an Uncivil Time; and the Biblical Insight to Tough Questions* series.

He has taught the philosophy of religion and apologetics at several seminaries. Dr. Denison serves as Resident Scholar for Ethics with Baylor Scott & White Health, where he addresses issues such as genetic medicine and reproductive science. He is a Senior Fellow with CEO Forum, 21st Century Wilberforce Initiative, the International Alliance of Christian Education, and Dallas Baptist University's Institute for Global Engagement.

He holds a Doctor of Philosophy and a Master of Divinity degree from Southwestern Baptist Theological Seminary. He also received an honorary Doctor of Divinity from Dallas Baptist University. Dr. Denison is the Theologian in Residence for the Baptist General Convention of Texas.

Prior to launching Denison Forum in 2009, he pastored churches in Texas and Georgia. Jim and his wife, Janet, have two married sons and four grandchildren.